# The
# LANGUAGE of EDUCATION

*Publication Number 409*
AMERICAN LECTURE SERIES®

*A Monograph in*
AMERICAN LECTURES IN PHILOSOPHY

*Edited by*
MARVIN FARBER, Ph.D.
*Distinguished Professor of Philosophy*
*State University of New York*
*at Buffalo*

It is the purpose of this series to give representation to all important tendencies and points of view in Philosophy, without any implied concurrence on the part of the Editor and Publisher.

# *The* LANGUAGE *of* EDUCATION

*Tenth Printing*

*By*

## ISRAEL SCHEFFLER

*Professor of Education and Philosophy*
*Harvard University*
*Cambridge, Massachusetts*

CHARLES C THOMAS · PUBLISHER

*Springfield · Illinois · U.S.A.*

*Published and Distributed Throughout the World by*
CHARLES C THOMAS • PUBLISHER
Bannerstone House
301-327 East Lawrence Avenue, Springfield, Illinois, U.S.A.

© *1960, by* CHARLES C THOMAS • PUBLISHER

ISBN 0-398-01656-9

Library of Congress Catalog Card Number: 60-11271

First Printing, 1960
Second Printing, 1962
Third Printing, 1964
Fourth Printing, 1965
Fifth Printing, 1966
Sixth Printing, 1966
Seventh Printing, 1968
Eighth Printing, 1971
Ninth Printing, 1974
Tenth Printing, 1978

*With* THOMAS BOOKS *careful attention is given to all details of manufacturing and design. It is the Publisher's desire to present books that are satisfactory as to their physical qualities and artistic possibilities and appropriate for their particular use.* THOMAS BOOKS *will be true to those laws of quality that assure a good name and good will.*

*Printed in the United States of America*
*R-1*

*To Samuel and Laurie
and their teachers*

# PREFACE

THE PURPOSE of this book is, through an application of philosophical methods, to clarify certain pervasive features of educational thought and argument. In particular, analyses of the logical force of educational definitions, slogans, and metaphors are presented, and a study is made of the central idea of teaching. It is hoped that the reflections to follow may be of interest not only to students of education and of philosophy but also to those who, as citizens or educators, are vitally concerned with the practice of the schools.

Several of the ideas here developed have grown out of my introductory lectures on the philosophy of education over the past few years and may perhaps be found useful in courses dealing with this subject. Many of those already acquainted with my recent anthology, *Philosophy and Education*, may find the present book convenient as an auxiliary, systematic treatment of certain related topics.

I wish to thank the editor and the publisher of *American Lectures in Philosophy* for their advice and cooperation. For numerous critical suggestions on form and content, I am indebted to Professors William K. Frankena, Sidney Morgenbesser, and Harold Weisberg. I am grateful to the John Simon Guggenheim Memorial Foundation for the award of a fellowship which enabled me to complete the final version of the study. I want to thank my wife for her encouragement and help in the preparation of the manuscript. Finally, I wish to acknowledge the stimulation I have received from my colleagues in education and in philosophy at Harvard, as well as from my students, who taught me while I taught them.

ISRAEL SCHEFFLER

# CONTENTS

# The
# LANGUAGE of EDUCATION

The following books have appeared thus far in this Series:

# INTRODUCTION

THIS BOOK is an effort in the philosophy of education. It deals first with certain recurrent forms of discourse related to schooling, and then offers an extended consideration of the concept of teaching, which is pervasive in such discourse. Through an analysis of selected statements in educational and social contexts, certain strategies are presented for the critical evaluation of statements of the same and related sorts, while study of the concept of teaching involves the treatment of such topics as the nature of educational rules, the relation of scientific research to schooling, the development of moral conduct, and the clarification of curricular discussion. Throughout the book, there is repeated emphasis on relating the critical evaluation of assertions to the contexts in which they appear, and further emphasis on disentangling practical and moral issues from others with which they are often confused. These two emphases, as well as several subsidiary notions employed, will be seen to be relevant to a greater variety of subjects than those specifically treated here.

To refer to this book as a study in the philosophy of education requires, however, some words of clarification. For there is an ambiguity in the notion of philosophical study that may prove misleading here unless explicitly resolved. This notion may, on the one hand, indicate inquiry into philosophical questions or the use of philosophical methods; it may, on the other hand, refer to historical study of what has been concluded by inquirers into philosophical questions or users of philosophical methods. These two sorts of enterprise are quite different in spite of the fact that they often bear the identical label. If we undertake the first sort of enterprise, we need, ourselves, to philosophize—that is, to take a stand on philo-

3

sophical issues or to apply philosophical tools of inquiry. If we undertake the second sort of enterprise, we do not, in the same sense, need to philosophize, but rather to try to understand the results and the course of past philosophizing.

The present study in educational philosophy is an effort of the first sort. It is an attempt to apply philosophical methods to fundamental educational ideas, rather than an attempt to chart the growth and career of received educational doctrines of a philosophical kind. Choice of the present course does not, however, rest upon a negative evaluation either of historical study or of philosophical doctrines of the past. An important and, indeed, necessary part of all philosophizing is a close study of the writings of past thinkers. It is, rather, the working attitude taken toward such writings that serves to distinguish the present attempt from studies in the history of ideas. The examination of such writings is, for present purposes, a tool rather than a primary aim. Thus, historically important views are here presented only in relation to problems receiving independent treatment, and no attempt will be made to provide a balanced historical narrative. That it is, however, not an undervaluation of history but only a particular working attitude toward historical doctrines that is here involved may perhaps be illustrated by consideration of the following, related question: What is the difference with respect to past scientific doctrines between the historian of science and the practicing scientist? It surely is not true that the one quotes his predecessors whereas the other does not. Nor is the one any less dependent, in general, on previous work in the field than the other. Rather, the historian studies past doctrines with the aim of understanding their genesis, development, and influence whereas the practicing scientist is primarily concerned with their bearing on current problems of independent scientific interest.

The distinction between philosophical inquiry and the history of ideas is here stressed not because it is presumed to be particularly subtle, but rather because it has not been sufficiently acknowledged in many recent presentations of philosophy of education. That the present occasion is, moreover, especially suited for a fresh emphasis on philosophical inquiry into education is indicated by the spurt of new and fruitful developments within philosophy as a whole, particularly in English-speaking countries.[1] To give an inkling of these developments, it is necessary to present a brief account of the course that philosophy has taken in recent years. Any brief account of such a large topic must be impressionistic and over-simplified, but not therefore unilluminating. Provided the following remarks are understood to represent a mere sketch of a rich and complex phenomenon, they may serve to introduce the reader to the contemporary climate of philosophical work.

Philosophy, in a word, may be said to seek general perspective, on a rational basis. Historically, those called 'philosophers' have concerned themselves with such subjects as the nature of the physical universe, mind, causality, life, virtue, law, good, history, and community. Historically, also, they have tried to argue rationally about such general topics and to defend their views by appeal to evidence and reasons open to all. The philosopher wants to see things in perspective and he wants to see things sharp and clear. He strives for a maximum of vision and a minimum of mystery.

In its quest for generality, philosophy thus bears a certain resemblance to religion, but differs from it in its exclusive appeal to rational argument, whereas religion appeals also to other sources of authority, such as revelation, sacred writings, and tradition. In philosophy's exclusive appeal to rational evidence, it resembles the sciences, but differs from them in being more general, in trying not only to understand the world through science, but also to comprehend science itself as a mode of understanding, as one aspect of a varied human experience.

The scope of each science, at any given time, is restricted in two ways. First, it is not and need not be concerned with relating its findings to the other special sciences nor to disparate realms such as those of the law, of practical life, of the arts, and of common sense. Secondly, it uses but does not itself generally analyze basic notions held in common with other domains, e.g., 'evidence,' 'theory,' 'cause,' 'purpose,' 'object.' The scientist, in short, takes over certain fundamental ideas and applies them in investigations legitimately abstracted both from other investigations and from other sorts of undertaking. These two sorts of restriction in scope are perfectly

1. In this connection, see Passmore, J.: *A Hundred Years of Philosophy*. London, Gerald Duckworth & Co. Ltd., 1957.

reasonable from the scientist's standpoint; indeed, they are not to be thought of as arbitrary limitations on his work but rather as conventions that render his energies effective through channelling them.

Yet, they leave room for another, characteristically philosophical, sort of enterprise. The philosopher may, that is, seek general perspective precisely in overriding the restrictions of scope proper to the special sciences. Thus, he may strive for generality either by building on accepted findings and common experiences in various domains in order to elaborate a picture of the whole world, or by analyzing the basic ideas and assumptions recurring in a variety of special fields. These two forms of the search for generality are familiar components of the philosophic tradition. They have, however, been unequally affected by the development of science in modern times.

With the increasing specialization of scientific knowledge and the amassing of data, it has become more and more difficult to encompass available information in a single, significant world-picture. Attempted world-pictures have thus increasingly run the practical risk of turning out superficial or badly inaccurate, though not theoretically shown to be incapable of providing significant illumination. Philosophers have thus naturally tended, in increasing numbers, to seek general perspective not by gathering the fruits of knowledge, but by analysis of the roots,—the basic concepts, assumptions, arguments, and inferences characteristic of different domains. Some philosophers have then proceeded to employ such analysis for the projection of an integrated picture, not of the universe, but of the human mind;[2] others have remained content with

2. See, for example, Cassirer, E.: *An Essay on Man.* New Haven, Yale University Press, 1944, and his statement, (p. 68) "Man's outstanding characteristic, his distinguishing mark, is not his metaphysical or physical nature—but his work. It is this work, it is the system of human activities, which defines and determines the circle of 'humanity.' Language, myth, religion, art, science, history are the constituents, the various sectors of this circle. A 'philosophy of man' would therefore be a philosophy which would give us insight into the fundamental structure of each of these human activities, and which at the same time would enable us to understand them as an organic whole." See also, in this connection, Langer, S. K.: *Philosophy in a New Key.* Cambridge, Harvard University Press, 1942; Reprinted by Penguin Books, Inc., First Pelican Books Edition, February, 1948.

clarification of the ideas themselves. The procedures and standards of analysis employed have also varied considerably. Yet, it is clear that the focus of philosophic attention has come, more and more, to center on basic concepts and modes of understanding rather than on the vast array of specialized bodies of information available for incorporation in any modern world-picture.

The development of science has, however, had an even more profound effect on the course of philosophy. It seemed to show that experimental methods are alone suitable for attaining knowledge of nature. Philosophy could no longer, it appeared, be plausibly construed as a kind of super-science, yielding nature's deepest secrets. Philosophers could no longer interpret their task as the deductive proof of factual theorems on the basis of self-evident axioms disclosed in intuition. Constrained, in the face of this challenge, to reinterpret their rôle and to offer some other, more acceptable, approach of their own, many philosophers began, indeed, by renouncing all claims to a superior intuition together with the professional right to make intuitive pronouncements about the world. They then proceeded to develop, as their basic task, the logical evaluation of assertions—the examination of ideas from the standpoint of clarity and the examination of arguments from the standpoint of validity.

This reorientation in rôle has fused with the emphasis on basic concepts, discussed earlier, to shape the characteristic posture of much contemporary philosophy. Such philosophy strives for general perspective through a study of the root ideas and arguments of various domains, applying and refining, for this purpose, a wide range of logical, linguistic and semantic tools. The rebirth and significant advance of logical studies at the turn of the century and the pioneer work of outstanding philosophers in its early decades served to provide the newer orientation with attractive models.[3] Philosophical analysis, in substantially its current forms, got under way—interested fundamentally in the clarification of basic notions and modes of argument rather than in synthesizing available beliefs into some total outlook, in thoroughly appraising root ideas rather than in painting suggestive but vague portraits of the universe.

3. See Passmore, J., Op. cit., especially chapters 5, 6, 9, 15, 18.

Such a conception of philosophy, though currently widespread, is not without deep roots in philosophical tradition. It has, indeed, been suggestively compared to the Socratic philosophy, depicted in Plato's dialogues as a search, through critical discussion, to achieve general understanding of a variety of root ideas. Like the Socratic philosophy, contemporary analysis is also in principle applicable to any subject-matter. It has, however, as a matter of historical fact, largely concentrated on scientific, mathematical, and ethical concepts since its twentieth-century beginnings. The reasons are difficult to be sure of. Undoubtedly, the example set by its pioneer thinkers played an important rôle, as did the traditionally central position of these concepts in the preoccupations of philosophers generally. Whatever the reasons, contemporary philosophical analysis has only fairly recently begun to be applied more broadly, to areas such as law, religion, social thought, and education.[4] Perhaps, as some critics have suggested, the narrower range and strongly methodological emphasis appropriate to a young and vigorous movement are giving way to the wider, substantive interests of maturity. However that may be, the prospects for philosophical inquiry into education, in the spirit of contemporary analysis and with the help of its methods, seem encouraging indeed. On the one hand, educators and educational theorists alike have, in recent years, increasingly affirmed the need for a critical re-thinking of the foundations of their subject; on the other hand, philosophy has increasingly devoted itself to the development and application of analytic instruments capable of assisting in such re-thinking.

What sort of landscape, then, does education present to the philosophical analyst? Among its central concepts are such fundamental ideas as 'knowing,' 'learning,' 'thinking,' 'understanding,' and 'explaining,' which figure prominently not only in the re-

4. See, for example, Flew, A., editor: *Essays on Logic and Language.* New York, Philosophical Library, 1951; Flew, A., editor: *Logic and Language* (Second Series). Oxford, Basil Blackwell, 1953; Laslett, P., editor: *Philosophy, Politics and Society.* Oxford, Basil Blackwell 1956; Scheffler, I., editor: *Philosophy and Education.* Boston, Allyn and Bacon, Inc., 1958; White, M.: *Religion, Politics and the Higher Learning.* Cambridge, Harvard University Press, 1959; Benn, S. I. and Peters, R. S.: *Social Principles and the Democratic State.* London, George, Allen, & Unwin, Ltd., 1959.

ceived philosophical literature, but in ordinary affairs and in scientific psychology as well. In addition, there are such more specifically educational ideas as 'mental discipline,' 'achievement,' 'curriculum,' 'character development,' and 'maturity,' which are intimately related to school affairs and are, moreover, foci of continuing practical debate. Such debate may serve to remind us that education is not only an abstract, intellectual matter but a field of practical endeavour and decision as well, in which institutional programs are put forth, criticized, justified, and rejected. The practical force of educational argument suggests, further, that educational ideas serve not only "descriptive" functions but also "policy" functions, so that widespread use of such terms as 'needs'. both in educational research and in debates over goals is as likely to facilitate confusion as simplification.[5] Educational discourse, in sum, embraces a number of different contexts, cutting across the scientific, the practical, and the ethical spheres, which lend a variety of colors and emphases to ostensibly common notions. A fundamental task of analysis would thus seem to be the disentangling of different contexts in which education is discussed and argued, and the consideration of basic ideas and appropriate logical criteria relevant to each.

This task is a large and complex one, and surely cannot be accomplished with anything like completeness in a single volume. The field which it defines requires sustained cultivation by many workers. It is thus only to selected aspects of the task that the present study is addressed, and its goal is, of course, not to say the last word on the topics treated, but rather to put forth analyses that may contribute to furthering critical reflection on the problems with which they deal. Nonetheless, the aspects selected for treatment were not chosen at random. They represent pervasive features of educational thinking and discussion, and it is hoped that their study may, accordingly, not only serve as a convenient philosophical starting-point, but may also be of some direct interest to educators and to others concerned with education. It is further hoped, as remarked earlier, that several of the distinctions and concepts introduced as instruments of the present analysis may

5. For relevant analyses of 'need,' see Archambault, R. D.: The concept of need and its relation to certain aspects of educational theory, *Harvard Educational Review*, 27:38, (Winter) 1957.

be found helpful in application to a wider range of areas than those here discussed.

The plan of the book is, then, as follows: In the next three chapters, three sorts of statement familiar in education are examined, with the view of logically appraising their status: statements of definition, educational slogans, and metaphorical descriptions. Statements of each of these sorts recur again and again in educational discussion, and are often treated quite uncritically in context. We shall attempt to analyze typical ways in which such statements are employed in typical circumstances, and to propose relevant principles for their critical evaluation. Our concern will thus not be to give a descriptive catalogue of actual definitions, slogans, and metaphors familiar in education, but rather to use certain of these as analytic examples for the presentation of strategies of logical appraisal.

The next two chapters are both concerned with the idea of 'teaching'. The first of these chapters is devoted to a general analysis of this idea and the outstanding ways in which it is used. The second of these chapters presents a comparison of 'teaching' and 'telling' that supplements the foregoing analysis, and offers some practical suggestions for clarifying discussions of the curriculum. The study as a whole thus falls into two main parts, the first, consisting of Chapters 1-3, dealing with certain recurrent types of statement in education and the second, consisting of Chapters 4 and 5, providing a connected treatment of a basic educational notion. The order in which the chapters should be read is, nevertheless, to a considerable extent, an individual matter. While the sequence of Chapters 4 and 5 represents a unit, it may well be taken, as a whole, before Chapters 1-3. Furthermore, the relatively greater difficulty of Chapter 1, as compared with Chapters 2 and 3, may make it desirable for some readers to attempt it after 2 and 3 rather than before.

## Chapter I

# DEFINITIONS IN EDUCATION

THE PRESENT chapter and the two to follow are concerned to evaluate the rôle played by three sorts of statement often encountered in discussions of education. These are statements of definition, statements embodying educational slogans, and statements containing metaphorical descriptions of education. Through a consideration of some typical contexts in which such statements occur, we shall attempt to clarify what may be called the logic of their operation in those contexts. Thus, although we shall make free reference to the social environment of these statements, our aim is not sociological. We are rather concerned to appraise the force of such statements when they appear in arguments—to examine the validity of conclusions drawn with their help and to propose ways in which their inferential uses may be relevantly criticized. These aims indicate in what sense our present purpose may be termed 'logical.' We turn now to a consideration of definition, which will occupy us for the rest of the chapter.[6]

It has already been remarked that educational discourse cuts across a variety of contexts in which different sorts of issues may be at stake, though identical terms reappear throughout. Thus, in introducing our treatment of the rôle of definitions, we must

6. There is a large literature on various aspects of definition. Some outstanding recent contributions are contained in Goodman, N.: *The Structure of Appearance*. Cambridge, Harvard University Press, 1951, Chapter I; Hempel, C. G.: *Fundamentals of Concept Formation in Empirical Science*. Chicago, The University of Chicago Press, 1952, Part I; Stevenson, C. L.: *Ethics and Language*. New Haven, Yale University Press, 1944, Chapter IX; Quine, W. V.: *From a Logical Point of View*. Cambridge, Harvard University Press, 1953.

not give the mistaken impression that there is some single way in which they are used in education. Rather, we must indicate at the outset, if only roughly, the sorts of context we have particularly in mind, leaving it to our further discussion to fill in relevant details.

We are here interested, broadly, in non-scientific discourses in which definitions of educational notions are offered, for example, in curriculum statements, in enunciations of program and objectives, in interpretations of education addressed to the general public, in debates over educational policy. It makes no difference whether the definitions offered in such contexts are put forward on scientific authority or not; the important fact is that they are presented not as technical statements interwoven with special scientific research and for theoretical purposes, but rather as general communications in a practical context.

The language of the sciences is not, to be sure, itself uniform in texture, and the forms of scientific expression vary widely with the progress of investigation as well as among the several branches of research. Nevertheless, the aim of science is, everywhere, to construct a network of theory adequate to all available facts, and the place of isolated statements in this network is, as a consequence, a rather secondary matter. Each such statement is constantly at the mercy of the scientist concerned to retain and increase the adequacy of the whole network in the face of accumulating information. Accordingly, no scientific statement is immune to radical alteration, change of rôle, or withdrawal in the interests of theoretical adequacy, no matter what the initial status of the statement may have been,—that is, no matter whether it was originally adopted as a definition, a hypothesis, a report, a law, or a theory. Thus, scientific definitions, in particular, are continuous with contemporaneous statements in their environing networks, and cannot well be evaluated in abstraction from these networks. Further, they are evaluated primarily in terms of their contributions to theoretical adequacy, irrespective of their degree of conformity to familiar usage, their ability to enlighten the layman, and their social and rhetorical effects. In sum, definitions in science are all, in an important sense, technical in purport and call for special knowledge and the use of special theoretical criteria in their evaluation. In scientific communications, definitions are presented and interpreted accordingly by professional members of the scientific community.

When such definitions are taken out of the context of professional research activity, however, and embodied in statements addressed to the public or to teachers or professionals of another sort, often in an institutional setting, they must be judged in this rôle as other definitions are judged in the same capacity. To say more exactly how various sorts of definition in this capacity are appropriately judged forms our present problem. We shall refer to them as 'general definitions'.

A general definition is often simply a stipulation to the effect that a given term is to be understood in a special way for the space of some discourse or throughout several discourses of a certain type. Such a definition may be called 'stipulative.' A stipulative definition exhibits some term to be defined and gives notice that it is to be taken as equivalent to some other exhibited term or description, within a particular context. It is a piece of terminological legislation that does not purport to reflect the previously accepted usage of the defined term,—if indeed there is such a predefinitional usage at all. Stipulative definitions may in turn be divided into two groups, depending on whether, in fact, the defined term has such a prior usage to begin with. Where it does not, the stipulative definition may be called an 'inventive' stipulation. Where, on the other hand, the stipulative definition legislates a new use for a term with a prior, accepted usage, it may be called a 'non-inventive' stipulation.

Inventive stipulation may be illustrated by the introduction of a system of arbitrary letters (e.g., 'S,' 'G,' 'E') to denote pupils' examination papers whose grades fall within specified intervals; these letters, having no accepted usage prior to their introduction, are assigned uses by stipulation. They are designated as shorthand labels equivalent to certain complicated descriptions of papers falling within the several score intervals. On the other hand, the use of a set of "qualitative" terms for the same purpose (e.g., 'passing,' 'fair,' etc.) is often governed by a series of non-inventive stipulations, non-inventive because such terms possess a predefinitional usage.[7]

To sum up the various categories of definition so far discussed, we began by segregating scientific definitions as recognizably special and technical in scope, and we labelled the rest 'general definitions.' Among general definitions, we next singled out stipulative definitions as laying down conventions for the interpretation of terms within certain contexts, without regard to familiar usage. Finally, we divided stipulative definitions into inventive and non-inventive types, depending on the novelty of the defined term.

What are some typical motives for the making of stipulative definitions? When something needs to be referred to in a particular context, for which available language provides, at best, the possibility of extended description, convenience is served by introducing an abbreviatory term. Thus, in the above examples, repeated description of the several test intervals is avoided by introducing the abbreviatory letters 'S,' 'G,' etc. or the abbreviatory adjectives 'passing,' 'fair,' etc. Or, to take our own discussion as an example, the classificatory terms introduced earlier, e.g., 'non-inventive stipulative definitions' etc., served to give us handy labels with which to refer to things that would otherwise require repeated complicated description. These terms were thus themselves introduced by stipulation, in order to facilitate our presentation. Such abbreviations are not theoretically essential inasmuch as what is said with their help may be said, though in a much more cumbersome way, without it. Nonetheless, the economy of utterance they permit is a powerful practical motive for their employment. They are thus familiar devices, in education as elsewhere.

Since the purpose of abbreviation can be accomplished by using either a familiar term in a special way or else a wholly new term, stipulative definitions abbreviate equally well in either way, and, as a matter of fact, both inventive and non-inventive stipulations

7. Another contrast between inventive and non-inventive stipulation is illustrated by alternative ways of labelling grades in an elementary school. Two fifth grades may, for example, be distinguished as 'Bright' and 'Normal,' or they may be assigned two different letters, initials of their respective teachers' names, precisely in order to avoid the unwanted suggestions carried by their "qualitative" alternatives. For discussion of this point and related questions, I am indebted to Dr. David V. Tiedeman.

abound. Whether the one or the other sort is to be chosen on a given occasion depends on other factors than mere abbreviating facility,—for example, on the availability of a familiar term that, by its suggestiveness, will be likely to stimulate memory without arousing unwanted associations, or on the need to keep an otherwise suitable familiar term free for other uses within the relevant context.

What is, however, fundamental with regard to all stipulative definitions is that they do not purport to reflect the predefinitional usage of the terms they define. They legislate conventions that may be more or less helpful in discussion, that may be consistently or inconsistently followed, that may be coherent or not, taken as a whole, but they can neither be fairly justified nor rejected by consideration of the accuracy with which they mirror predefinitional usage. Once it is established that a stipulative definition or set of such definitions is formally coherent and pragmatically well-chosen, it is irrelevant to argue against it further on the ground that it fails to reflect the normal meaning of the defined term or terms. *In this special sense*, stipulative definitions may be said to be matters of arbitrary choice.

There is, however, another sort of general definition, which we here call 'descriptive' in contrast with the stipulative sort. Descriptive definitions, like the latter, may also serve to embody conventions governing discussions, but they always purport, in addition, to explain the defined terms by giving an account of their prior usage. In fact, descriptive definitions are thus often presented in answer to requests for clarification. The question, "What does that term mean?" is typically intended to elicit some explanatory rule or description of the term's prior functioning, that is, something in the nature of a descriptive definition. Every such definition is construable as a formula equating a defined term with other, defining, terms in a way that purports to mirror predefinitional usage. It is such mirroring that, it is hoped, will provide understanding of the defined term's meaning. An illustration is the definition of the term 'indoctrination' as 'the presentation of issues as if they had but one side to them.'[8] This and analogous definitions

8. This example is taken from Brubacher, J. S.: *Modern Philosophies of Education*. Second Edition. New York, McGraw-Hill Book Company, Inc., 1950, p. 201.

of 'indoctrination' are frequently presented in an attempt to clarify the term as it is ordinarily and most clearly applied. Such definitions aim at the distillation of a general rule out of the term's prior usage, a rule that may at once sum up such usage and clarify it by relating it to the usage of other, familiar terms, a rule that may thus be employed to teach someone how the term is normally used.

In contrast to stipulative definitions, then, descriptive definitions are not simply abbreviatory devices adopted for convenience and theoretically eliminable. They purport not to economize utterance, but to provide explanatory accounts of meaning. As a result, there is no counterpart among descriptive definitions to the inventive stipulation, inasmuch as the terms defined by inventive stipulation have no prior meanings to be explained. Given, however, a term *with* a prior use, the non-inventive stipulation may put it to unfamiliar uses for the purpose of facilitating communication, whereas the descriptive definition may provide a general account of its prior use. If we visualize the definition as a formula, after the fashion of modern logic, in which the defined term (definiendum) appears at the left and the defining term or set of terms (definiens) appears at the right separated by some special sign ('=df') in the middle, (e.g., 'indoctrination =df the presentation of issues as if they had but one side to them'), then we may also visualize the difference between stipulative and descriptive definitions as a difference in the *direction* of interest in the formula as a whole. Whereas the interest in stipulation moves from right to left, that is, toward more condensed utterance with increased vocabulary, the interest in descriptive definition moves from left to right, i.e., toward expanded explanatory utterance with a smaller vocabulary.

It is evident that descriptive definitions are not matters of arbitrary choice in the way in which stipulative definitions have been said to be. For beyond formal and pragmatic considerations, descriptive definitions may be called to account in respect of the accuracy with which they reflect normal predefinitional usage. It is not irrelevant to argue against a descriptive definition that it violates such usage. It may indeed be explicitly stipulated that the term 'tree' is to count as equivalent to 'window' for the duration of some particular discussion, but such an equation clearly violates the prior use of the term 'tree' and must hence be judged wrong if it is offered rather as a descriptive definition. This example may, incidentally, serve to underscore the fact that a given definitional equation may serve either as a stipulation or as a descriptive definition, depending on the context in which it is offered and the purposes which it is intended to serve; the difference is thus not a formal or purely linguistic one but relates rather to the pragmatic environment of the definition. If and only if the definitional equation purports to mirror predefinitional usage is it descriptive.

The mirroring of predefinitional usage is, we have said, explanatory of the terms defined. The level and mode of attempted explanation vary, however, considerably. Descriptive definitions may be offered in the hope of helping someone to apply the defined term with proficiency. They may be offered rather as means of acquainting someone with the reference of the defined term, though not in the hope of enabling him thereby to apply the term to instances, much as the term 'virus' might be defined to a high school class. They may be formulated in cases where the term is already being applied proficiently to instances, the point being to distill the guiding principle of such application and to show its interconnection with others. This last sort of enterprise is characteristically philosophical, exemplified in the work of many thinkers since Socrates, whose attempt was precisely to formulate general characterizations covering known instances of important terms. This enterprise, is, however, by no means limited to philosophers, occurring again and again in systematic explanations of various subject matters, including education.

The relation of descriptive definition to prior usage requires certain additional remarks, postponed until now for purposes of simplification. It must not be supposed that the prior usage of any given term is consistent and exhaustive. To begin with, ordinary terms are often ambiguous, so that descriptive definitions require to be supplemented, if only by context, with some indication of the usage taken to be relevant. For example, the term 'trunk' applies in some contexts to certain boxes and in other contexts to certain portions of the anatomy of elephants, but in no context to both.

Further, even after elimination of ambiguities, prior usage normally does not cover every instance to be faced. It clearly rules every term applicable or inapplicable to some instances, but leaves the rest undecided; in this sense it is not exhaustive. For example, the word 'chair' clearly applies to certain objects in accord with standard usage, e.g., the four-legged, straight-backed, movable pieces of wooden furniture placed around the dinner table and used for seating adults. It also clearly does not apply to a number of other objects, e.g., windows, horses, engines, lakes, and clouds. But some things are neither clear cases of application nor clear cases of non-application, e.g., toys resembling chairs but made of plastic and two and a half inches high, and objects used for seating adults but lacking the typical shape of chairs, for example, boxes or barrels. Regarding such undecided or borderline cases, descriptive definitions are free to rule either way. Thus, for such a definition to be accurate, it must accord with prior usage only in the sense of not violating clear instances of such usage. That is, where prior usage clearly applies a term to some object, the definition may not withhold it; where prior usage clearly withholds the term from some object, the definition may not apply it. But with respect to undecided cases, the definition may serve to legislate in any manner. Thus, though every clear predefinitional application or non-application of a given term provides a condition of accuracy to be met by descriptive definitions of the term, not every application decreed by such a definition is governed by some predefinitional condition of accuracy. The demands of accuracy allow considerable leeway to descriptive definition.

We have, then, so far distinguished two broad types of general definition, the stipulative type not purporting to accord with prior usage but only to facilitate discourse, and the descriptive type purporting to explain terms by providing an account of their prior usage. We have remarked that, though formal considerations are relevant in the appraisal of a definition of either type, only descriptive definitions may appropriately be criticized for failure to accord with predefinitional usage. We noted, therefore, that the process of stipulative definition is unrestricted in a special way in which descriptive definition is not, though even the latter leaves considerable room for variation within the bounds of accuracy.

It remains for us now to consider a further, practical rôle of general definitions that is of especial importance in education; it is through this practical rôle that general definitions are often keyed fairly directly into social practices and habits of mind. How may the practical rôle of general definitions be described? Roughly speaking, some terms (e.g., the term 'profession') single out things toward which social practice is oriented in a certain way. (This orientation may be supposed expressible by a general principle of action: Example: "All professions ought to receive privileged treatment.") To propose a definition that now assigns such a term to some new thing may in context be a way of conveying that this new thing ought to be accorded the sort of practical treatment given to things hitherto referred to by the term in question. (E.g., to define 'profession' so as to apply to a new occupation may be a way of conveying that this new occupation ought to be accorded privileged treatment.) Similarly, to propose a definition that withholds such a term from an object to which it has hitherto applied may be a way of conveying that the object in question ought no longer to be treated as the things referred to by the given term have been treated. Even if a definition is proposed that assigns the term just exactly to the objects to which it has hitherto applied and to no others, the point at stake may be to defend the propriety of the current practical orientation to such objects and to no others, rather than (or as well as) to mirror predefinitional usage.

Where a definition purports to do either of these three things, it is acting as an expression of a practical program and we shall call it 'programmatic.' As in the case of stipulative and descriptive definitions, programmatic definitions are not recognizable as such by their linguistic form alone; reference to the context needs to be made. A definition may, for example, have the effect of implying some practical consequence in *hypothetical* combination with *some* principle of action, but this does not mean it is therefore programmatic. It may not, that is, purport to convey the practical consequence in question; the context may make it clear that the definition is not to serve as a practical premise. Thus it is the practical purport of the definition *on a particular occasion* that reveals its programmatic character. The same repeatable formula, obviously, may be programmatic on one occasion and not on the next. A programmatic definition, in effect, may perhaps be said to convey the practical consequence itself, rather than merely to express a premise capable of yielding it under suitable conditions. It is this practical force of some definitions on particular occasions that is of interest to us here.

Programmatic definitions represent the last sort of general definition that will be distinguished for our present purposes.[9] Thus, together with the stipulative and descriptive sorts, programmatic definitions exhaust the class of general definitions here discussed. The difference between each sort and the others, as has already been emphasized, is not a formal difference. Exactly the same definitional equation may be stipulative, descriptive, or programmatic, depending on the context in which it is offered.

What sorts of consideration are relevant to the appraisal of programmatic definitions? Let us consider a partly schematic example. Imagine a type of work $W$ that has hitherto fallen clearly outside the range of the term 'profession.' Suppose a definition is offered that has the consequence of applying this term to $W$. From the context, it is evident that the definition is not being used merely to introduce an eliminable, abbreviatory device to facilitate communication. Proposals of other likely abbreviations are, for example, uniformly rejected. Further, when the objection is raised that the defi-

9. The treatment of definition in the text is influenced in several respects by the important work of C. L. Stevenson, op. cit., but the use of the term 'programmatic' rather than his term 'persuasive' is motivated by certain substantive considerations marking a difference of approach: Persuasive definitions are interpreted by Stevenson in terms of emotive meaning, that is, in terms of psychological responses, feelings and attitudes, whereas programmatic definitions are here interpreted in terms of the orientation of social practice. The treatment in the present text connects the practical force of definitions with the *references* of constituent terms, and associated principles of action, rather than with the emotive properties of the terms themselves. This practical force is thus not explained as a conscious or unconscious use of definition "in an effort to secure, by this interplay between emotive and descriptive meaning, a redirection of people's attitudes" (Stevenson, op. cit., p. 210) but appears as a "cognitive" effect, a function of the references and logical relations between terms and statements involved. Emphasis on persuasiveness suggests that where a definition goes beyond the explanatory function, its surplus function is not to raise new questions but rather to cause new effects in the hearer. Emphasis on programmatic character, on the other hand, suggests that the bearings of a definition on social practice frequently are expressible as *arguable issues*, though they are not issues of meaning but practical or moral questions. The emphasis on programmatic rather than persuasive definitions is not a denial of the importance of the latter, but, at least in part, an attempt to stress the "cognitive" import of definitions for social practice, which has, it seems to me, been unduly neglected recently despite its significant rôle in general discourse.

nition fails to accord with prior usage, its author is unperturbed; he wants precisely to depart from such usage. It thus becomes clear that the definition is neither stipulative nor descriptive. The author's point is different; he wants $W$ to be treated as other sorts of work are treated which fall within the predefinitional range of the term 'profession.' This point is one that requires independent, practical evaluation. It would surely be irrelevant to argue that the definition is not a very helpful abbreviatory convention, or that it is unorthodox with respect to predefinitional usage. What needs investigation is the practical or moral question: "Ought $W$ to be accorded the treatment normally given to sorts of work hitherto called 'professions'?" The considerations appropriate to this question are relevant to the appraisal of the definition itself.[10]

From the preceding discussion, it is clear that, though programmatic definitions are like stipulative ones in not being bound by prior usage, they are unlike stipulations in raising moral or practical issues. Even stipulations, we have already remarked, are not *wholly* arbitrary. They may be criticized in terms of formal considerations, such as those relating to consistency, and appraised with regard to their helpfulness as devices of communication, e.g., do they aid memory, do they mislead by introducing irrelevant associations, etc. But they do not raise moral issues which go beyond the immediate discussion; they do not call for evaluation of practice, for appraisal of commitments, for the making of extra-linguistic decisions. In general, it is thus a mistake to suppose that *any* definition is wholly arbitrary, and an even more serious mistake to suppose that all but the descriptive definitions are bound only by considerations of consistency and communicatory convenience. Programmatic definitions, in particular, may be used to express serious moral choices.

Programmatic definitions, it may then be said, are like descriptive definitions in raising questions that go beyond those of consistency and convenience. But the kind of question that is raised by either sort of definition differs strikingly from the kind of question raised

10. For treatment of related questions see Cogan, M. L.: The problem of defining a profession, *Annals of the American Academy of Political and Social Science*, 297:105, (January) 1955; Cogan, M. L.: Toward a definition of profession, *Harvard Educational Review*, 23:33, (Winter) 1953; and Lieberman, M.: *Education as a Profession*. Englewood Cliffs, N. J., Prentice-Hall, Inc., 1956.

by the other. On the one hand, the issue is whether or not the definition before us accords with prior linguistic usage; on the other hand, the issue is whether or not the program expressed by the definition ought to be adopted.

We may now sum up the comparison of our three sorts of general definition by labelling, in a rough way, the interest underlying each sort. The interest of stipulative definitions is communicatory, that is to say, they are offered in the hope of facilitating discourse; the interest of descriptive definitions is explanatory, that is, they purport to clarify the normal application of terms; the interest of programmatic definitions is moral, that is, they are intended to embody programs of action.

There is obviously no point at all in pitting these three sorts of general definition against each other or any or all of them against scientific definitions. The purposes each serves are all perfectly legitimate and there is no call to decide for or against some set or to rank them all in some scale of value. Rather, what is wanted is that the critical appraisal of a definition of any sort be directed to the issues at stake on the occasion of its use, and to this end the foregoing distinctions among sorts of definitions may be helpful.

There are, however, certain complications to be faced in considering the relations among sorts of general definition. It has been stressed above that the same definitional equation or formula may, on different occasions, express a stipulative, descriptive, or programmatic definition, depending on the context. May there, in addition, be an overlapping of definitional sorts on the same occasion, and for the same definitional formula? May the same definition, in context, belong to more than one sort?

If we consider this possibility first for stipulative and descriptive definitions, we find that overlapping is excluded. Descriptive definitions purport to describe predefinitional usage whereas stipulative definitions do not. Thus, no given definitional equation can be both stipulative and descriptive at the same time.

How about an overlap of stipulative and programmatic sorts? If we consider first inventive stipulation, it seems again that the possibility is excluded, inasmuch as the defined term in such a case, having no prior application at all, cannot, *a fortiori*, single out objects toward which practice is oriented in some particular way. Thus, a definition of such a term cannot express a program by suggesting either an alteration or a perpetuation of the practice associated with it. Nor, if the defining phrase denotes objects uniformly associated with some practical orientation, can the defined term serve to suggest an alteration or perpetuation of such orientation. For in order to do that, it should have to possess some initial application of its own that differed from or matched that of the defining phrase. But such initial application is just what is lacking in inventive stipulation.

On the other hand, when we examine the possibility of an overlap of non-inventive stipulation and programmatic definition on a given occasion, it is evident that such overlap does frequently occur. Furthermore, it is evident why it occurs, at least on numerous occasions. Briefly, the expression of a particular program may call for new linguistic apparatus; a given definition may, at one stroke, create such apparatus as well as give voice to the program. Examples abound in writings on social topics, but one educational illustration must here suffice.

We often find, in recent writings on education, that the term 'curriculum' is defined as referring to the totality of experiences of each learner under the influence of the school.[11] Now this definition has been rightly criticized as vague and difficult in a number of respects, but the point that concerns us here is quite different. The definition, it should be noted, has as an intended consequence that no two pupils ever have the same curriculum and, further, that no two schools ever have the same curriculum, each school having as many curricula as it has pupils. These consequences clearly violate the standard predefinitional usage of the term 'curriculum.' For such usage surely allows us to speak truly of the (unique) curriculum of a given school, of a number of schools with the same curric-

11. Compare the article 'Curriculum Development,' contributed by O. I. Frederick, in Monroe, W. S., editor: *Encyclopedia of Educational Research*. New York, The Macmillan Company, 1941, which states that "in recent educational literature and in this report the school curriculum is considered to be all the actual experiences of the pupils under the influence of the school. From this point of view each pupil's curriculum is to some extent different from that of every other pupil. The course of study is considered to be a suggestive written guide for teachers to use as an aid in curriculum planning and teaching." (Passage cited with permission of the Macmillan Company.)

ulum, and of the curriculum of a school as enduring for a longer or shorter interval during which its pupil population is completely changed.

This definition is not an inventive stipulation, for the term 'curriculum' does have a prior usage, as we have just seen. Nor is it merely a descriptive definition that happens to be unsuccessful, a defective attempt to mirror predefinitional usage. For if the violations of such usage that we have noted are made explicit, they are not treated as if they were counter-instances to a proposed descriptive hypothesis. Rather, they are typically taken as further symptoms of the definition's intended distinctiveness, which is then usually supported by other arguments. These arguments generally make it plain that the definition is programmatic, that its point is precisely to apply the familiar term in a strange way, in order to re-channel the practice associated with it. In particular, the programmatic point is to extend the school's responsibility, hitherto limited to its so-called formal course of study, in such a way as to embrace the individual social and psychological development of its pupils. The presentation of this programmatic point, however, requires repeated reference to the enlarged domain of responsibility envisaged, and, to facilitate such reference, the same definition stipulates the appropriate novel use of the term 'curriculum.' Thus the definition serves, on the same occasion, both as programmatic and as stipulative, in the non-inventive sense. Indeed, the need for the stipulation in question arises out of the program espoused.

In evaluating this double-purpose definition, it is clearly beside the point to dwell on its violation of predefinitional usage. Rather, the definition must be appraised as programmatic and as stipulative simultaneously. We have to ask both the practical question, "Ought the school's responsibility to embrace the individual social and psychological development of its pupils?", and the linguistic question, "Is the stipulated use of the term 'curriculum' consistent and convenient for the purposes of the author's discussion?" Neither question alone is sufficient for the appraisal of the definition, for a positive answer might be forthcoming to one but not to the other. We might, that is, agree that the program is sound, without agreeing that the stipulation is consistent and helpful for the discussion at hand. We might, more seriously, agree that the stipulation is formally sound and convenient for purposes of the author's discussion, but feel that the program expressed is wrong. In order to allow for such important divergences, both questions need to be asked with respect to definitions of the sort we have been considering.

It is clear, then, that if the author of such a definition succeeds in showing that his program is sound, he has not thereby shown that his stipulations are helpful. Nor, surely, if he concentrates on showing how helpful his stipulations are in his discourse, is he supporting in any way whatever the worthwhileness of the program expressed. Both the linguistic and the moral or practical issues need to be independently considered.

Frequently, however, in cases of an overlap of stipulative and programmatic sorts of definition, arguments proceed at cross-purposes because such need is in fact forgotten. Thus, critics of the above-mentioned definition of 'curriculum' have often concentrated on pointing out its vagueness and various other difficulties, while defenders have often countered with moral commendation of the program conveyed by it. There are, nevertheless, in the case of definitions with stipulative and programmatic overlap, certain typical features which help to remind us of the need for a double evaluation. Thus, the stipulative character of these definitions is usually evident from explicit cues in the context, e.g., the definition may be introduced expressly as a convention for the purpose of facilitating discussion and there is, in any event, no attempt to justify it by reference to predefinitional usage. Further, the very fact that such usage is normally altered by these (non-inventive) definitions suggests that they may have another point, in particular, a practical one. We are, in effect, put on our guard by the very strangeness of the usage stipulated, and led to ask whether it might not be true that more than just stipulation is involved.

This latter built-in aid to memory is generally not available in the remaining, and perhaps most interesting, case of overlap that we still need to examine, i.e., the case of definitions that are simultaneously descriptive and programmatic. Obviously, there will here be no contextual cues appropriate to stipulations; furthermore, while the evidence given of correspondence with prior usage may be sketchy, the claim of correspondence with such usage will normally be clearly made. There may, to be sure, be actual violations of prior usage by descriptive definitions—when they are inaccurate. For it must be remembered that descriptive definitions are those *purporting* to mirror predefinitional usage accurately, and some such definitions fail to accomplish what they claim. Inaccurate descriptive definitions will thus, in fact, also provide violations of prior usage that may (it will perhaps be said) remind us of the possibility of programmatic interpretation. But our belief that such inaccuracy is unintended renders it less likely to put us on our guard and to suggest a quite different, i.e., programmatic, interpretation; the definition seems after all, just a purported descriptive formula that has failed. It is perhaps because the violation of prior usage here offers no reliable cue to suggest programmatic interpretation that cases of descriptive-programmatic overlap are so often misconstrued and, hence, sources of confusion in arguments on social matters. Let us now turn to the examination of such overlap.

We have already noted that a definition which assigns a given term to just those things to which it has hitherto applied and to no others may still be expressing a program. Suppose, for example, that someone wishes to oppose the program expressed by the 'curriculum' definition we considered earlier. Whereas that definition departed from the prior use of the term, thus conveying the desirability of expanding the school's responsibility, it would be most natural to express opposition to such expansion by propounding a counter definition that accurately mirrored prior usage and purported to do so, that, in effect, restricted the curriculum to the school's formal course of study. Both parties would, in such a case, be agreeing on the principle that the school is responsible for the curriculum, but, in construing the *scope* of the curriculum differently, they would be counselling different practices on the part of the school.

This is, of course, not the only way such a difference of practical programs may be expressed. The opponent of expansion might, for instance, let the stipulated sense of 'curriculum' stand. He might then formulate his opposition to the expressed program by denying the assumption that the school is responsible for the whole curriculum. Conversely, the proponent of expanded responsibility need not express his program through stipulative definition. He might, for example, let the term 'curriculum' retain its usual application, and go on to argue that the school is responsible for more than just the curriculum. (Compare, e.g., the term 'extra-curricular activities.') Nevertheless, so long as both parties retain the principle that the curriculum is coextensive with the school's responsibility, their differing definitions may be vehicles for the expression of contrary educational programs. If this is indeed what is at stake in a given debate, it is important not to suppose that, because the opposing views are couched in definitional form, the issue is merely a verbal one.

Whether or not such a debate is programmatic in a given case is, again, not merely a formal question, to be determined by inspection simply of what is said. Much depends on the context in which the debate takes place, on the manner in which it is conducted, on the practical principles presupposed, on the willingness of the participants to accept certain reformulations of their positions, on the likelihood that the definitions are to serve as practical premises, and so forth. It may be difficult in particular cases to decide whether the issue at stake is descriptive alone or programmatic as well. In such cases, it is wise to adopt the stronger assumption that the issue is both descriptive and programmatic, and to evaluate the debate in both ways.

We have considered one example of descriptive-programmatic overlap, then—indeed, a case in which the definition is descriptively accurate as well, and in which it is opposed programmatically to a non-inventive stipulation. In this example, as before, two questions have to be asked of the descriptive definition—the practical question, "Ought the school's responsibility to exclude the individual social and psychological development of its pupils?" and the linguistic question, "Does the definition accurately mirror the predefinitional use of the term 'curriculum'?" These questions are, as before, logically independent, and a positive answer to the one has no force at all with respect to the other. In particular, even if the definition is in fact linguistically accurate or correct, nothing whatsoever is established concerning the expressed program.

We turn now to another sort of example of descriptive-programmatic overlap, one in which undecided instances are involved and in which two equally accurate definitions may yet be programmatically opposed. It will be recalled that we earlier noted the existence of borderline instances, to which the prior usage of a term neither clearly applies nor fails to apply the term in question. We remarked that with respect to such borderline instances, descriptive definitions are free to rule either way without impairment of their accuracy. They may thus, in effect, serve to legislate new usage as well as to describe prior usage. (In fact, it is doubtful that any accurate descriptive definition can fail to legislate in this way.) It follows that alternative definitions that are equally correct in describing the prior usage of a term may differ among themselves in legislating for hitherto undecided cases. If the undecided cases in question involve *alternatives of practice*, the point at issue may well be programmatic. We shall illustrate this situation presently.

It is important, however, at this point to make especial note of the fact that alternative accurate definitions are possible, and that it must therefore not be supposed that to each term there corresponds one and only one correct definition. Nor is this the case only for general definitions. In science, indeed, the rivalry of alternative accurate definitions (at least with respect to scientific usage) often occurs. Sometimes, the choice in such cases makes no scientific difference and can hence be arbitrarily made. Sometimes, the choice is decided in terms of theoretical simplicity or convenience, rather than the desirability of assimilating borderline cases to one group of instances rather than another. Sometimes, however, such desirability does enter as a consideration and the relevant question here becomes, "How ought these borderline cases to be regarded for scientific purposes?" This, if you like, is a question of practice in one broad sense, but it is a question that is independent of social policy and moral considerations, and so falls outside the range of practice as we have here been construing it.

In the case of general definitions, however, such independence cannot be taken for granted. The decision over borderline cases may, in fact, be precisely the place where programmatic differences come to a head. Moreover, unlike the previous example in which an accurate descriptive definition was opposed to a stipulation that clearly violated prior usage, programmatic opposition on borderline cases may be embodied in rival definitions whose accuracy is beyond question. We are now ready to turn to some examples.

Legal contexts provide clear instances of definitions that legislate on practical matters while purporting to sum up prior (legal) usage.

Suppose a new sect is founded, with no prescribed creed or holy book, but with recommended rituals and hymns, and meetings designed to improve men's conduct and ethical attitudes. Ought this sect to be called 'religious'? Prior usage may be puzzled, but whether the legal definition to be adopted has the effect of applying the term to this sect or not will determine whether or not it will receive those privileges the law accords to religious institutions. Two definitions of 'religion,' equally correct in that each adequately covers clear cases of predefinitional usage, may still diverge in the way in which they classify our imagined sect. So far as the standard, prior meaning of the term 'religion' is concerned, both these definitions are correct; neither can be said to be superior to the other in respect of considerations of meaning alone.

It is clear that these definitions in legal contexts are programmatic in nature as well as descriptive, their point being to direct practical policy with respect to the new case, as well as to summarize past usage. To choose one of these definitions, we should have to go outside the realm of considerations of meaning and appeal to other sorts of considerations, e.g., those of a moral and practical kind. We should have to ask, for example, "Are the social consequences of classifying the new sect as 'religious' more or less desirable than those of classifying it as 'non-religious'?" The issue involved here is clearly not a verbal but a moral and practical one, to be decided on moral and practical grounds. It would be a bad mistake to establish the descriptive accuracy of some proposed definition and then to try to settle the moral issue by appeal to the definition alone.

Definitional questions of the sort we have just considered arise recurrently in the law and in social thought generally. Their presence is often strikingly obvious where social change confronts us with borderline instances of our received social terms, instances that urgently require adjudication. Consider, for example, the problems of redefining 'property,' 'economic rights,' etc., under unprecedented conditions of industrialism, or the new conquest of space. Our social terms, we may say, reflect the familiar social environment with reference to which our principles of action have become crystallized; new social decisions may be expressed by redefining such terms so as to enable our received rules to cope with a changed environment. As mentioned earlier in another connection, the expression of such decisions need not in every case be achieved through redefinition; nevertheless, redefinition is often employed to this end, and is hence programmatic in such instances.

The important point that emerges from reflection on these examples is that appeal to the accuracy of definitions, even when it is fully warranted, cannot itself support any controversial program that may be involved in applying the definition to borderline cases. Many thinkers have claimed to possess special insight into the real and unique meanings of social terms, on the basis of which they could decide what ought to be done in controversial social spheres. Knowing the uniquely real definitions of 'the state,' 'society,' 'man,' etc., they have supposed that they could derive therefrom social imperatives governing newly arisen conditions requiring decision. If our previous analysis is correct, their claim is totally misguided. For, in the first place, there are alternative ways of descriptively defining 'the state,' 'society,' 'man,' etc., all equally accurate with respect to prior usage or meaning, but differing in their legislation of new cases. In the second place, moreover, there is always the possibility of altering even prior standard usage in order to convey a practical program. (We have illustrated this possibility in discussing the overlap of non-inventive stipulation and programmatic definition in the case of the term 'curriculum.') In the third place, finally, definitions of social terms do not in isolation yield practical consequences at all; they require contextual supplementation by principles of action. (In the 'curriculum' case, recall, for example, the principle that the curriculum is coextensive with the school's responsibility.) Only in relation to such principles do social definitions serve to convey practical consequences. There is, then, always the possibility of countering such consequences by accepting the definition as accurate and denying the presupposed practical principles. In short, the jump from definition to action is long and hazardous, even where the definition is unquestionably accurate as an account of meaning.[12]

The above considerations are highly relevant to the use of definitions in discussions of education. To offer a definition of the term 'education,' for example, in non-scientific contexts is quite often to convey a program as well as, at best, to state an equation that may be accurate with respect to prior usage. Even where such a definition is accurate, *such accuracy cannot be used as a measure of the worth of the expressed educational program.* Different programs are compatible with accuracy and the justification of any program is thus an independent matter.

Definitions of terms in education are, to be sure, not generally embedded in as precise a network of practical rules as are legal definitions, but, in combination with broad and informal (though socially fundamental) principles of action, they often serve nevertheless as vehicles for debating new programs of education, new views of method, aims, or content. We have already seen one example in the case of the term 'curriculum.' Definitions in education thus may be said to resemble definitions in art which, though of no legal significance, also serve frequently to express changing conceptions of the artist's task.[13] For example, definitions of artistic innovators often extend the use of the term 'work of art' to new sorts of objects; the counter definitions of conservatives withhold the term from these same objects. Both sets of definitions are, furthermore, often consonant with artistic tradition, that is, they are in conformity with prior usage. The dispute can thus not be taken, in such cases, to be a matter of the meaning of terms alone. Rather, it is a question of divergent artistic programs, conveyed by opposing programmatic definitions that are also descriptively accurate. An attempt to define a work of art is not, in the words of Collingwood, "an attempt to investigate and expound eternal verities concerning the nature of an eternal object called Art," but rather to give "the solution of certain problems arising out of the situation in which artists find themselves here and now."[14]

12. Karl Popper, in his work, *The Open Society and its Enemies.* Third edition. London, Routledge & Kegan Paul Ltd., 1957 (First edition, 1945), has strongly criticized what he calls 'essentialism,' the search for essential meanings of basic terms; the present paragraph in the text is indebted to his treatment. Nevertheless, the present text diverges from Popper's defence of the exclusively abbreviatory function of definitions, in that we here allow for descriptive definitions with explanatory force. Essentialism is nonetheless avoided in that an extensional interpretation of descriptive definition is adopted throughout, allowing for different accurate definitions of each notion.

13. For the points made in this paragraph, I am indebted to Ziff, P.: The task of defining a work of art, *The Philosophical Review,* 62:58, (January) 1953.

14. Collingwood, R. G.: *The Principles of Art.* Oxford at the Clarendon Press, 1938, p. vi, quoted in Ziff, Op. cit.

Education, like art, literature, and other phases of social life, has changing styles and problems in response to changing conditions. These conditions require decisions governing our practical orientation to them. Such decisions may be embodied in revision of our principles of action or our definitions of relevant terms or both. In the making of new definitions for such purposes, there is no special insight into meanings that tells us how revisions and extensions are to be made. Not an inspection of the uniquely real meanings of terms (if this were possible) is here relevant, but an investigation in the light of our commitments, of the practical alternatives open to us as well as of alternative ways of putting desired decisions into effect.

The way in which this point is often overlooked in professional writings on education may be illustrated by the following description of a new program for secondary schooling:

> "The curriculum was organized around four sorts of activities, story projects, hand projects, play projects, and excursion projects; opportunity was provided for continuing evaluation of activities, and such evaluation was directed by pupils. The organization of this school program proceeded naturally from the belief that the fundamental meaning of the concept of education is to help boys and girls to active participation in the world around them."

The issue is here put in terms of fundamental meanings. But, in fact, what is at stake? Clear cases of the concept 'education' as embodied in usage prior to the advent of modern innovations did not include cases where play and excursions as well as pupils' continuing evaluation characterized the educational program. But some of the clear cases, like the present example, did involve special institutions, overall direction by adults, evaluation of achievement, and so forth. The present educational innovation, as a matter of fact, is both sufficiently like and sufficiently unlike clear past instances to constitute a borderline case.

To propose an educational reform along the lines of the above passage is to say that such a procedure ought to be tried under the aegis of the schools. The proposal may thus be said to assimilate the borderline case to the past clear cases, leaving intact all those principles of action formulating our positive orientation to educational endeavor. The stated definition tries to do just that by, in effect, dwelling on the resemblances, i.e., on the common aim to help boys and girls to active participation in the world around them. It would, however, be easy to concoct alternative definitions that built on the differences, segregating the new reform from previous clear cases of 'education.' The issue, in short, is one of practice, and needs evaluation in terms of our preferences and commitments as well as in terms of expected effects. What is to be done with respect to this proposed educational reform is thus our practical responsibility and cannot be decided by inspection of the concept of 'education.'

Let us now consider a final example of a somewhat more abstract sort. In educational discussions, it is often said that a definition of 'man' provides directions for curriculum making and for evaluation of methods of schooling.[15] It is, indeed, true that the way in which we organize our educational efforts and operate our schools is conditioned by prevalent definitions of human nature. It is not, as we have seen, that practical educational consequences are derivable from accurate definitions taken in isolation but rather that they may be conveyed by such definitions in contexts where relevant principles of action are taken for granted. The conclusion often drawn in educational theory is that we must first decide what the correct definition of 'man' is, and that then practical educational consequences will only need to be inferred by us through the application of pure logic.

This picture is, however, wrong not only in postulating a simple deductive implication between definitions of human nature and practical educational consequences, but also in failing to take account of the several points noted above regarding definitions that are both descriptive and programmatic. There are an indefinite number of alternative definitions of 'man,' indefinitely many ways of dimensionalizing his structure and capacities, all equally accurate. To choose one such dimensionalization on the basis of its accuracy and to proceed to read off curricular counterparts to each

15. In this connection see, for example, Ducasse, C. J.: What can philosophy contribute to educational theory?, *Harvard Educational Review*, 28:285, (Fall) 1958. Ducasse asks what the several dimensions of man's nature are, as a preliminary to determining the chief dimensions of education, which (as he says) "correspond, of course, to those of man's nature."

dimension, as is often done, is to beg the whole question. One basis of choice of a definition for educational purposes must be a consideration of the very consequences for educational practice to be expected as a result of adoption of such a definition. The programmatic character of such a definition means that it requires evaluation with respect to the program conveyed. Indeed, such evaluation may even lead us to adopt a non-inventive stipulation that clearly violates prior usage; it surely may lead us to differentiate between equally accurate descriptive definitions that convey different programs. It is just because definitions of the latter sort are programmatic that their adoption should follow rather than precede a moral and practical evaluation of the programs they convey. Inspection of meanings cannot substitute for such an evaluation.

An analogous point holds for the transfer of definitions from science to education, a transfer whose dangers we have already intimated. We remarked that scientific definitions are continuous with the theories and evidence in their respective domains, and that they may therefore best be treated apart. They cannot be fitted into our stipulative, descriptive, and programmatic categories without serious distortion. They are to be judged, roughly, by their contribution to the adequacy of their respective scientific networks in accounting for the facts. It follows that, to take a scientific definition for programmatic use is not to avoid the need for evaluation of the program such use conveys. The scientific adequacy of a definition is no more a sign of the practical worthwhileness of such a program than accuracy with respect to prior usage.

Finally, note must be taken of the converse truth. Just as, if a definition is accurate it does not automatically follow that its associated program is worthwhile, so if a definition is inaccurate, it does not automatically follow that its program is not worthwhile. We have already seen, in the case of non-inventive stipulative definitions that are also programmatic, the possibility of a worthwhile program conveyed by a descriptively inaccurate formula. Nevertheless, writers occasionally do argue, invalidly, that their definitions are accurate, since their programs are worthwhile, and they provoke the equally invalid rejoinder that their programs cannot be worthwhile since their definitions are inaccurate. The issue thus set up needs cutting through rather than intensified partisanship. It needs to be recognized, in short, that the same definitional formula on a given occasion may be both descriptive and programmatic, and that it thus requires double evaluation.

## Chapter II

# EDUCATIONAL SLOGANS

EDUCATIONAL slogans are clearly unlike definitions in a number of ways. They are altogether unsystematic, less solemn in manner, more popular, to be repeated warmly or reassuringly rather than pondered gravely. They do not figure importantly in the exposition of educational theories. They have no standard form and they make no claim either to facilitate discourse or to explain the meanings of terms. We speak of definitions as clarifying, but not of slogans; slogans may be rousing, but not definitions.

Slogans in education provide rallying symbols of the key ideas and attitudes of educational movements. They both express and foster community of spirit, attracting new adherents and providing reassurance and strength to veterans. They are thus analogous to religious and political slogans and, like these, products of the party spirit. Since slogans make no claim to facilitate communication or to reflect meanings, some of the main points of the last chapter are here irrelevant. No one defends his favorite slogan as a helpful stipulation or as an accurate reflection of the meanings of its constituent terms. It is thus idle to criticize a slogan for formal inadequacy or for inaccuracy in the transcription of usage.

There is, nevertheless, an important analogy with definitions, that needs to be discussed. Slogans, we have said, provide rallying symbols of the key ideas and attitudes of movements, ideas, and attitudes that may be more fully and literally expressed elsewhere. With the passage of time, however, slogans are often increasingly interpreted more literally both by adherents and by critics of the movements they represent. They are taken more and more as literal

36

doctrines or arguments, rather than merely as rallying symbols. When this happens in a given case, it becomes important to evaluate the slogan both as a straightforward assertion and as a symbol of a practical social movement, without, moreover, confusing the one with the other. In the need for this dual evaluation lies the analogy mentioned between slogans and definitions.

In education, such dual evaluation is perhaps even more important than in the case of political and religious slogans, for, at least in Western countries, educators are not subject to the discipline of an official doctrine and are not organized in creedal units as are religious and political groups.[16] Educational ideas formulated in careful, and often difficult, writings soon become influential among teachers in popularized versions. No official discipline or leadership preserves the initial doctrines or some elaboration of them, seeing to it that they take precedence over popular versions at critical junctures, as is familiar in religion and politics. Educational slogans often evolve into operational doctrines in their own right, inviting and deserving criticism as such. It is important to remember, at this point, that though such criticism is fully warranted, it needs to be supplemented by independent criticism of the practical movements giving birth to the slogans in question, as well as of their parent doctrines. We may summarize by saying that what is required is a critique both of the literal and the practical purport of slogans; parent doctrines must, furthermore, be independently evaluated.

The example of John Dewey's educational influence is instructive. His systematic, careful, and qualified statements soon were translated into striking fragments serving as slogans for the new progressive tendencies in American education. Dewey himself criticized the uses to which some of his ideas were put,[17] and his criticisms had the effect of inviting reconsideration and reflection. He was, after all, the acknowledged intellectual leader of the movement. Increasingly, however, progressive slogans have taken on a life of their own. They have been defended as literal statements

16. I am, it should be obvious, not arguing for the desirability of such disciplined organization, but only suggesting that its lack renders more urgent the dual criticism of slogans.

17. Dewey, J.: *Experience and Education.* New York, The Macmillan Company, 1938.

and attacked as such. Critics, in particular, have often begun by attributing the literal defects of progressive slogans to Dewey's parent doctrines and gone on to imply that the progressive movement has thereby been shown unworthy in its aims and operation.

That the literal purport and practical purport of slogans require independent criticism may be illustrated by consideration of the slogan, "We teach children, not subjects." In view of the fact that this and closely analogous formulas have sometimes been treated as literal statements, and not merely as rallying symbols of the progressive movement, let us examine the statement literally. Does it make sense?

Suppose I told you I had been teaching my son all afternoon yesterday. You would have a perfect right to ask, "What have you been teaching him?" You would not necessarily expect some single type of answer, such as the name of some academic subject. If, instead of saying, "Mathematics," I were to answer, "How to play first base," or "To be polite," or "The importance of being earnest," you would be satisfied. But, suppose, in answer to your question, I said, "Oh, nothing in particular, I've just been teaching him, that's all," you would, I think, be at a loss to understand how we spent the afternoon. It would be as if you had asked me, "What did you have for dinner?" and got the reply, "Oh, nothing, I've just had dinner, but had nothing *for* dinner."

I might, of course, say reasonably in the latter case, "I can't recall," or "I don't know the name of the dish," or "I don't think I can describe it to you." But in each such case, I am acknowledging that your question has some true answer naming or describing some food, though I am, for one or another reason, not supplying it. To say, however, "I had nothing *for* dinner, just had dinner," is to deny that your question has such a true answer in this case, and it is this denial that makes the assertion impossible to understand. Analogously, to revert to the teaching example, I might, of course, say, "I can't recall the name of the book," or "I don't know the name of the swimming stroke," or even "I don't think I can describe it to you now" (suppose it is a complicated chess strategy). If, however, I said none of these things but insisted rather that I had been teaching the boy nothing, you would fail to understand me, or, at least, fail to take me as uttering a literal truth.

This case must be distinguished from another in which you ask me, "What have you taught him?" that is, "What have you been successful in teaching him?" In answer to this question, it is quite possible for me to say, "Nothing." It is quite possible for me to have been teaching algebra to someone to whom I have been unsuccessful in teaching algebra. I have taught him nothing, though I have been teaching him algebra, I have been trying to get him to learn algebra but he has failed to learn. To ask, however, in the words of our original question, "What have you been teaching him?" is not to ask, "What is it that you have been successful in teaching him?" It is rather to ask, "What have you been trying to get him to learn?" As to this question, if I answered, "Nothing; I have just been teaching him, but have not been trying to get him to learn anything at all," you would, I think, be really puzzled. It would be as bad as if I had said, "I spent yesterday afternoon teaching swimming." and in response to your question, "To whom?" I had replied, "Oh, to no one; just teaching swimming, that's all." If no one teaches anything unless he teaches it to someone, it is equally true that no one can be engaged in teaching anyone without being engaged in teaching him something.

Let us return now to the statement, "We teach children, not subjects." If we take 'subjects' as a general word without restriction to academic subjects, it appears that the statement is not interpretable as both literal and true, since it seems to say, quite literally, "We teach children, but there isn't anything that we try to get them to learn." We have, indeed, previously seen that a denial that anything is taught is legitimate where the question concerns the success of teaching rather than its intent. But this fact is surely of no help in interpreting the slogan before us, as the resulting statement in such an interpretation would be, "We teach children, but we are not successful in teaching them anything." The latter statement, unlikely in any event, would hardly be claimed true by proponents of any educational movement. Taken literally, the slogan is a clear failure, and cannot be used as a serious premise in any argument.

To reach this conclusion, however, is not to evaluate the practical purport of the slogan, the aims it symbolized, the educational tendencies with which it was associated. What, in fact, was its practical purport? Briefly, its point was to direct attention to the child, to relax educational rigidity and formalism, to free the processes of schooling from undue preoccupation with adult standards and outlooks and from mechanical modes of teaching, to encourage increased imagination, sympathy and understanding of the child's world on the part of the teacher. To know the educational context in which such a practical message took shape is to grasp the relevance of its emphasis. Conversely, the relevance of the message cannot be seen without reference to the context. The story is a long one but a quotation from a recent study will serve to indicate the outstanding features. Citing Joseph Rice's report on the American public schools in 1892, based on a tour of 36 cities in which Rice talked with 1,200 teachers, L. A. Cremin writes:[18]

> "Rice's story bore all the earmarks of the journalism destined to make 'muckraking' a household word in America. In city after city public apathy, political interference, corruption, and incompetence were conspiring to ruin the schools . . . A principal in New York, asked whether students were allowed to move their heads, answered: 'Why should they look behind when the teacher is in front of them?' A Chicago teacher, rehearsing her pupils in a 'concert drill,' harangued them with the command: 'Don't stop to think, tell me what you know!' In Philadelphia, the 'ward bosses' controlled the appointment of teachers and principals; in Buffalo, the city superintendent was the single supervising officer for seven hundred teachers. With alarming frequency the story was the same: political hacks hiring untrained teachers who blindly led their innocent charges in sing-song drill, rote repetition, and meaningless verbiage."

Given such a situation, the relevance of a renewed educational emphasis on the world of the child is obvious. It is, moreover, easy to see that a positive evaluation of this emphasis, representing the practical purport of our slogan,[19] is altogether independent of the

18. Cremin, L. A.: The progressive movement in American education: a perspective, *Harvard Educational Review*, 27:251, (Fall) 1957.
19. By the relevance of a slogan's practical purport, I mean its applicability within the context of its use on a particular occasion. In speaking of the evaluation or warrant of this practical purport, I refer to the question whether or not such application ought indeed to be made. To illustrate, compare the case of imperatives. Consider the imperative, 'Put on the light!', uttered on a given occasion. It is relevant on that occasion only if the light is not already on. Even if it is relevant, however, we may still ask whether or not the light ought to be put on.

criticisms we made of its literal sense. That is, one commits no logical error in accepting these criticisms and at the same time applauding the emphasis of the slogan. Whether or not one is to applaud this emphasis is a separate question, requiring consideration of practical and moral issues in relation to some given context. It is, finally, clear that the practical relevance of a slogan, as well as the applause accorded to it, may vary with context quite independently of its literal purport. In the case of the slogan before us, many feel, indeed, that its practical message is presently less urgent that it once may have been, that it is either irrelevant or considerably less warranted in the current educational situation. This variation in the fortunes of the slogan's practical purport is a function of changing times and changing problems; it cannot result from the failure of the slogan as a literal doctrine, which is invariant.

One important corollary is that doctrines that contradict each other as literal statements may nevertheless, in their practical purport, represent abstractly compatible emphases which may, to be sure, vary independently in relevance and moral warrant from context to context. That is, there may be no cause for supposing that we have an irreconcilable conflict of practical proposals of which we must flatly reject at least one. This point may be illustrated by considering a statement that has acquired the typical status of a slogan in education, the statement that there can be no teaching without learning. As there can be no selling without buying, so there can be no teaching without learning. A recent writer[20] has argued against this statement, asking us to consider as a counter-example the case of a teacher who has tried his best to teach his pupils a certain lesson but has failed to get them to learn it. Shall we say that such a man has not, in fact, been teaching, has not earned

20. Broudy, H. S. *Building a Philosophy of Education.* Englewood Cliffs, N. J., Prentice-Hall, Inc., 1954, p. 14. Broudy writes, "Many educators rather glibly pronounce the dictum: 'If there is no learning, there is no teaching.' This is a way of speaking because no educator really believes it to be true, or if he did he would in all honesty refuse to take most of his salary. There is a difference between successful teaching and unsuccessful teaching, just as there is a difference between successful surgery and unsuccessful surgery . . . To teach is deliberately to try to promote certain learnings. When other factors intrude to prevent such learnings, the teaching fails. Sometimes the factors are in the teacher; sometimes in the pupil; sometimes in the very air both breathe, but as long as the effort was there, there was teaching."

his pay, has not fulfilled his responsibility? Surely this case shows that there can be teaching without learning.

If we take the two statements, "There can be no teaching without learning," and "There can be teaching without learning," simply as literal doctrines, we must agree that they are contradictory. Further, we must agree that the counterexample produced against the first of these statements is effective in showing it to be false. If we have an actual case before us of teaching without learning, then we must reject the doctrine that denies the existence of such cases. The counterexample does, moreover, represent a real case of teaching without learning. Here, in short, does seem to be a flat contradiction between two statements, one of which is wrong.

It is, furthermore, easy to see why the statement, "There can be no teaching without learning," sounds so plausible as a literal doctrine, though it is in fact false. For though in some uses of the verb 'to teach' it does not imply success, in others it does. We have already noted the difference between asking, "What have you been teaching him?" ("What have you been trying to get him to learn?") and "What have you taught him?" ("What have you been successful in teaching him?"). The first question, we may say, contains an "intentional" use of the verb, while the second contains a "success" use.[21] It is clear that if the pupil I have been teaching has in fact not learned anything, I may reply to the second question (but not to the first) by saying, "Nothing." For the second question, that is, unless my pupil has learned something, I cannot say I have taught him anything, i.e., there can (here and in all "success" uses) indeed be no teaching without learning.

Some further illustrations may be helpful, especially since the distinction between "success" and "intentional" uses is important and will recur in later discussions. Clearly, if I have been teaching my nephew how to catch a baseball, he may still not have learned, and may in fact never learn, how to catch a baseball. I have, of course, been trying to get him to learn how to catch a baseball, but I need not have succeeded. Generally, then, we may say that the schema "X has been teaching Y how to . . ." does not

---

21. I am indebted to the treatment of achievement words in Ryle, G.: *The Concept of Mind*. London, Hutchinson's University Library, 1949. See also Anscombe, G.E.M.: *Intention*. Oxford, Basil Blackwell, 1957.

imply success. Suppose, however, that I have taught my nephew how to catch a baseball. If I have indeed taught him, then he must, in fact, have learned how. Were I to say, "Today I taught him how to catch a baseball but he hasn't learned and never will," I would normally be thought to be saying something puzzling. We may, then, say that the schema "X taught Y how to . . ." does imply success. This schema represents a "success" use of 'to teach' whereas the earlier schema does not, representing rather an "intentional" use of the verb.

It should be noted, incidentally, that not every use of the simple past tense of the verb implies success, though the above "success" schema contains such a form. It is, for example, true that some teachers taught mathematics last year to some students who learned nothing of mathematics. It should further be noticed that "success" uses of the verb 'to teach' do not eliminate distinctions of relative proficiency. To have been successful in teaching implies no more than that students have learned in relevant ways, not that they have become masters. We may ask rhetorically, in traffic, "Who taught *him* to drive?" suggesting that, though he has learned, he is not very good at it. It is minimal achievement, sufficient to warrant us in saying that learning has occurred at all, that is normally implied by "success" uses of the verb 'to teach.'

Finally, we should make note of the fact that 'to teach' is not exceptional in having both "success" and "intentional" uses. Indeed, many verbs relating to action have both uses inasmuch as what is done is often described in terms of trying to reach a goal, the attainment of which defines the success of the try. To say a man is building a house does not mean he has succeeded or ever will. He is, of course, doing something with a certain intention and certain hopes and beliefs; he is, in short, trying to bring it about or make it true that there be a house built by himself. It may, further, be normally understood that what he is doing in this attempt is reasonably considered effective. But from the fact that someone is building a house it cannot be inferred that there is (or will be) some house built by him. He may have been building ("intentional" use) until the flood came and wiped away his work, and he then never completed the job. He may thus never have built ("success" use) the house that he had been building ("intentional" use). Or, better, there may never exist any house built ("success" use) by him, though he has, in fact, been house-building ("intentional" use).

If now, with respect to the verb 'to teach,' we recognise that it has both "intentional" and "success" uses, we see that for the latter uses, there can, indeed, be no teaching without learning. If one's examples are all drawn from such uses, the doctrine that there can be no teaching without learning seems entirely plausible. Nevertheless, the general way in which it is expressed leaves the doctrine open to falsification through a single counterexample, such as has been discussed above. Thus we return, after a long digression, to the conclusion we reached earlier: taken as literal doctrines, the statements, "There can be no teaching without learning," and "There can be teaching without learning" are contradictory, hence irreconcilable, and it is the first statement, moreover, that must be rejected.

If, however, we examine the practical purport of these two statements, it becomes clear that, though their practical emphases are not equally relevant and warranted in every context, neither are they opposed as exclusive alternatives. Rather, they relate to different practical aims that are perfectly compatible. The practical purport of the statement "There can be no teaching without learning" is closely related to that of the slogan "We teach children, not subjects," that is, to turn the attention of the teacher toward the child. But we have here a distinctive emphasis on the child's learning as the intended *result* of teaching, the point being to improve the effectiveness of teaching by referring it to its actual as compared with its intended results. This emphasis hardly strikes anyone today as being either very original or very controversial. It seems rather taken for granted in quite prosaic contexts. Imagine someone saying to a soap manufacturer, "Look here, you'd really do a better job if you systematically studied your product and tried to improve it. You can't really call yourself a soap manufacturer unless you produce good soap, and you can't do that unless you look at what you're turning out and make sure that it is up to par." Such a little speech would seem rather out of place in our consumer-oriented world. Soap makers are looking at their products anyway (not, perhaps, always to make better soap, but at least to make soap more attractive to buyers). No soap maker supposes that, apart from their contribution to his final product, his manufacturing processes have any intrinsic value.

But teachers often have supposed something dangerously like this. They often assume that, apart from their effects on students, their teaching in just the way they habitually do has intrinsic value, and is therefore self-justifying. Instead of achieving attainable improvements through deliberate effort, they thus tend to deny that any improvements are needed or possible so long as they continue to teach as before. When such educational inertia is widespread, as it seemed to many observers to be when our slogan gained currency, the practical purport of the slogan may seem urgent, indeed, revolutionary. To speak, moreover, of teaching as selling and of learning as buying, to suggest that teaching be compared with business methods improvable by reference to effects on the consumer, was to signal strikingly the intent to support reform of teaching.

In part because such reform has become widespread, the practical purport of our slogan appears to many current observers irrelevant or less warranted. Indeed, it has seemed to such observers that the pendulum has in many places swung too far in the direction of orientation to the child's world and preoccupation with the effects of teaching on this world. The schools have, in some respects, been described as too much concerned with their consumers. Teachers, feeling the weight of each student's adjustment and personality conflicts resting on their tired shoulders, have in many instances tried to do too much—to become parents, counselors, and pals as well as teachers. They have, (understandably, given such aspirations coupled with the emphasis on consequences) felt harried and guilty at not being able to do all that their charges require, accepting meanwhile the responsibility for all failures in learning upon themselves.[22]

If someone should want to help the morale of such teachers, he would hardly keep repeating the old message under the new conditions. Rather, he would want to say, "Stop feeling guilty, give up your attempts at omnipotence, stop paying so much attention to the inner problems and motivations of your students. Do your very

22. See Freud, A.: The rôle of the teacher, *Harvard Educational Review*, 22:229, (Fall) 1952, and Riesman, D.: Teachers amid changing expectations, *Harvard Educational Review*, 24:106, (Spring) 1954.

best in teaching your subject and testing your students and when you've done that, relax with an easy conscience." This represents just the practical purport of the statement, "There *can* be teaching without learning." It is this emphasis which seems to many current writers relevant and warranted in the present situation.

Both emphases, however,—that of the present statement and that of its opposite—are abstractly compatible in spite of the fact that they may be unequally relevant or warranted in specific educational contexts. It is, thus, possible to hold (and, indeed, to urge) that teaching ought to be appraised and modified in the light of its effects on learners, and at the same time to believe (and to stress) that there are limits to what the teacher can do, with the best will in the world: whatever he does, he may still fail to achieve the desired learning on the part of his pupils.

In given situations, however, it may be considered more important to maintain the teacher's morale by stressing the limits of his responsibility than to try to improve teaching by stressing the need to examine effects. Whether we say "Try to improve!" or "Don't worry, you've done your best!" is indeed, in this way, a function of the context. But these emphases are not, in general, irreconcilable, nor do they require a flat rejection of the one or the other. They may, in fact, occur together and they may alternate in urgency. To sum up, when slogans are taken literally, they deserve literal criticism. We need, independently however, to evaluate their practical purport in reference to their changing contexts, as well as the parent doctrines from which they have sprung. We must, moreover, avoid assuming that when slogans are in literal contradiction to each other, they represent practical proposals that are in irreconcilable conflict.

## Chapter III

# EDUCATIONAL METAPHORS

IF WE compare metaphors with definitions and slogans, some contrasts are immediately apparent. Metaphors are not normally intended to express the meanings of terms used, either in standard or in stipulated ways. Rather, they point to what are conceived to be significant parallels, analogies, similarities within the subject-matter of the discourse itself. Metaphorical statements often express significant and surprising truths, unlike stipulations which express no truths at all, and unlike descriptive definitions, which normally fail to surprise. Though frequently, like programmatic definitions, conveying programs, metaphors do so always by suggesting some objective analogy, purporting to state truths discovered in the phenomena before us. Like slogans in being unsystematic and lacking a standard form of expression, they nevertheless have a much more serious theoretical rôle. They cannot generally be considered as mere fragments crystallizing the key attitudes of some social movement, or symbolizing explicit parent doctrines. Rather, they figure in serious theoretical statements themselves, as fundamental components.

The line, even in science, between serious theory and metaphor, is a thin one if it can be drawn at all. To say, "This table is composed of electrons," is clearly (at least) to invite comparison of the table and aggregates of tiny particles whose behavior is further elaborated in other statements. To be sure, the initial metaphor must lead to refinements in the comparison, expressed literally, and to experimental confirmation of predictions or other inferences derived from them. But the same holds true of theories generally, and there is no obvious point at which we must say, "Here the metaphors stop and the theories begin." In education, too, metaphorical statements are frequently found in key theoretical contexts as well as in policy contexts. What do they convey and how? We shall proceed from some general remarks to a consideration of selected educational metaphors.

Generally, we may regard the metaphorical statement as indicating that there is an important analogy between two things, without saying explicitly in what the analogy consists. Now, every two things are analogous in some respect, but not every such respect is important. Still, the notion of importance varies with the situation: what is important in science may not be important in politics or art, for example. If a given metaphorical statement is to be judged worthwhile or apt, the analogy suggested must be important with respect to criteria relevant to the context of its utterance.

Further, the metaphorical statement does not actually state the analogy, even where a relevantly important one exists. It is rather in the nature of an invitation to search for one, and is in part judged by how well such a search is rewarded. Again, the pattern is similar to that of a theory or, if you like, a theoretical hunch. It is no wonder, then, that metaphors have often been said to organize reflection and explanation in scientific and philosophical contexts. In practical contexts too, metaphors often serve, analogously to programmatic definition, as ways of channelling action, though always by purporting to indicate that some important analogy may be found within the relevant subject-matter.

Aside from independent evaluation of programs that may be conveyed by particular metaphorical assertions, metaphors may be criticized in roughly two ways. First, we may reach the conclusion that a given metaphor is trivial or sterile, indicating analogies that are, in context, unimportant. Second, we may determine the limitations of a given metaphor, the points at which the analogies it indicates break down. Every metaphor is limited in this way, giving only a certain perspective on its subject, which may be supplemented by other perspectives. Such limitation is no more reason to reject a metaphor completely than is the fact that alternative theories always exist in itself a reason to reject any given theory in science. Nevertheless, a comparison of alternative metaphors may be as illuminating as a comparison of alternative theories, in indicating the many-faceted character of the subject. Such a comparison may also provide a fresh sense of the uniqueness of the subject, for to know in what ways something is like many different things is to know a good deal about what makes it distinctive, different from each. Lastly, where a particular metaphor is dominant, comparison helps in determining its limitations, and in opening up fresh possibilities of thought and action. In the rest of the chapter, we shall be concerned to make such a comparison of common metaphorical ways of speaking about education.

Max Black suggests that the familiar growth metaphor is one that lends itself to the expression of revolt against educational authoritarianism.[23] How does this happen? There is an obvious analogy between the growing child and the growing plant, between the gardener and the teacher. In both cases, the developing organism goes through phases that are relatively independent of the efforts of gardener or teacher. In both cases, however, the development may be helped or hindered by these efforts. For both, the work of caring for such development would seem to depend on knowledge of the laws regulating the succession of phases. In neither case is the gardener or the teacher indispensable to the development of the organism and, after they leave, the organism continues to mature. They are both concerned to help the organism flourish, to care for its welfare by providing optimum conditions for the operation of laws of nature. The growth metaphor in itself thus embodies a modest conception of the teacher's rôle, which is to study and then indirectly to help the development of the child, rather than to shape him into some preconceived form, a contrary metaphor which we shall presently consider.

Where does the growth metaphor break down? It does seem plausible with respect to certain aspects of the development of children, that is, the biological or constitutional aspects. Regarding these, we can pretty well say, roughly, what sequences of stages may be normally expected, and how the passage from stage to stage may be helped or hindered by deliberate effort on the part of others. Where such knowledge is lacking concerning details, it may presumably be furnished by further investigation. The nature and order

23. Black, M.: Education as art and discipline, *Ethics*, 54:290, 1944, reprinted in Scheffler, I.: *Philosophy and Education*, Op. cit.

of these stages of physical and temperamental development, and of the capacities for behavior they make possible are, indeed, relatively independent of the action of other individuals, though even here cultural factors make their impact.

If we once ask, however, how these capacities are to be exercised, toward what the temperamental energy of the child is to be directed, what sorts of conduct and what types of sensitivity are to be fostered, we begin to see the limits of the growth metaphor. The sequence of physical and temperamental stages is, in fact, quite compatible with any number of conflicting answers to these questions. For these aspects of development, there are no independent sequences of stages pointing to a single state of maturity. That is why, with regard to these aspects, it makes no literal sense to say, "Let us develop all of the potentialities of every child." They conflict and so cannot all be developed. To develop some is to thwart others. To withdraw is not to allow nature's wisdom full scope, but to decide in one way rather than another, where both are compatible with nature; responsibility for such decision cannot be evaded.

It has often been remarked that to think of history as if it were a plant, whose development through natural stages can only be facilitated or retarded by individuals, is a way of evading responsibility for affecting social events through choice and action.[24] It should be even more obvious that the course of children's social, cultural, and moral development is not divided into natural stages which cannot be fundamentally altered by others. It is clear that adults — parents and teachers — do more than simply facilitate the child's development toward a unique stage of cultural maturity.

It is the latter insight that underlies another familiar educational metaphor, that of shaping, forming, or molding. The child, in one variant of this metaphor, is clay and the teacher imposes a fixed mold on this clay, shaping it to the specifications of the mold. The teacher's initiative, power, and responsibility are here brought into sharp focus. For the final shape of the clay is wholly a product of his choice of a given mold. There is no independent progression toward any given shape, as there is with respect to the growth of

24. See, in this connection, Popper, K., Op. cit., and Popper, K.: *The Poverty of Historicism*. London, Routledge & Kegan Paul, 1957.

acorns, for example. Nor is there any mold to which the clay will
not conform. The clay neither selects nor rejects any sequence of
stages or any final shape for itself. The one choosing the mold is
wholly responsible for the result.

In the light of our previous remarks on the growth metaphor, it
is clear that this molding metaphor does not fit the biological-
temperamental development of the child, which is not alterable
throughout by adult action. The molding metaphor does, however,
seem more appropriate than the growth metaphor as regards cultural, personal, and moral development, which is, to a greater
extent, dependent on the character of the adult social environment.

But even here, the molding metaphor has its limitations. In the.
case of the clay, the final shape is wholly a function of the mold
chosen. The clay neither selects nor rejects any given mold. The
clay is, further, homogeneous throughout, and thoroughly plastic.
The shape of the mold is fixed before the molding process and remains constant throughout. Each of these points represents a dis-
similarity with respect to teaching. For, even if there are no laws
of cultural, moral, and personal development, there are nevertheless limits imposed by the nature of the pupils upon the range of
developments possible. These limits say what *cannot* be done with
the material rather than what *will* develop. Human nature does
not automatically select, but it rejects some forms that adults may
choose for it. Further, these limits vary from student to student
and from group to group. The student population is not thoroughly
homogeneous nor thoroughly plastic. Thus, if the educator's decisions are not made for him by nature, neither are they unlimited
by nature, and a study of these limits may make his decisions
wiser. Finally, if the teacher is indeed to pay attention to the nature
of his students, he will modify his methods and aims in the course
of his teaching and in response to the process itself. His teaching
is, then, not comparable to a fixed mold, but rather to a plan modi-
fiable by its own attempted execution.

It is the latter features of teaching that are accentuated in what
may be called the art metaphor in any of several forms, for example, that relating to sculpture. The sculptor's statue does not grow
of itself out of the rock, requiring only the artist's nurture; the
artist exercises real choice in its production, yet his initial block

of marble is not wholly receptive to any idea he may wish to impose on it. It rejects some of these by its internal structure. Neither is every block of marble like every other. Each block requires individual study of its individual capacities and limitations. Finally, the artist's initial idea is not one that is fully formed in advance, remaining fixed throughout. It gets the process started, but is ordinarily modified by the process itself, during which the artist is continuously learning as well as creating.

This sculpture metaphor seems particularly apt with respect to the features just described, but it cannot be said that it is perfect, or even better in every way than the ones previously considered. For example, the growth metaphor at least acknowledges the continuing development of the object in question after the departure of the gardener, whereas the sculpture metaphor does not; the statue ceases to grow when the sculptor is finished with it. Nor is the teacher, unlike the sculptor, bound only by aesthetic standards. His aims and his methods are subject to moral and practical criticism as well.

Thus, it seems mistaken to try to find a progressive order of metaphors in education, each metaphor more adequate and comprehensive than the last. Here the comparison of such metaphors with scientific theories itself breaks down. Educational metaphors in general use are of help in reflecting and organizing social thought and practice with respect to schooling, but they are not tied in with processes of experimental confirmation and prediction. They thus do not develop cumulatively as do scientific theoretical frameworks. They are rather to be thought of, perhaps, as ranged around their common subject, whose individual complex of features may be illumined by a comparative examination of the metaphors.

The analogy indicated by a given metaphor may, as suggested earlier, be important in one context but not in another. A good metaphor is thus not generally good in every context. This fact is important for our present discussion, since education, as we have stressed, is the common ground of a variety of contexts. It is thus wise to be critical about accepting metaphors in a given context that have proved illuminating elsewhere, even though it is the same subject that is involved in both cases. The transplantation of metaphors may, indeed, be misleading inasmuch as it may blur distinctions vital in the new context though unimportant in the old.

The effects of such transplantation may be illustrated by reference to a widespread metaphorical account of education that is clearly related to the growth metaphor but is more inclusive; we will here call it the 'organic metaphor.' There are numerous variants and uses of this metaphor in educational writings; we shall here give a brief description for the purposes of discussion.[25] Culture, in the anthropological sense in which it comprises the mores, folkways, technology, social organization, language, law, ideology, science, and art of a given society, is taken as analogous to life in the individual organism. Just as living things are different from inanimate things in maintaining themselves by renewal, in reacting to external forces so as to retain their equilibrium with the environment, using these forces as means of further growth, so cultures retain their continuity by reacting to external forces in such a way as to maintain their equilibrium and to grow adaptively and creatively. Though individual life ends with the death of the individual, cultural life does not. Just as the individual's several cells and tissues die and are replaced while his life goes on, so the culture's "cells," that is, its individual members, die and are replaced without destroying the life of the culture. The cells in each case do not all die simultaneously but rather continuously, and they are continuously replaced. The processes by which new physical cells replace the old in the individual organism are responsible for preserving biological continuity. The processes by which new members of a culture replace the old guarantee cultural continuity. These latter processes constitute education, whose function is to transmit the culture's life from the group to each new member, thus renewing it continuously.

Now the organic metaphor resting on the above analogies assimilates education to the processes by which individuals take on

25. This description is suggested by Dewey, J.: *Democracy and Education*. New York, The Macmillan Company, 1916, Chapter I. In summarizing the chapter, Dewey writes, for example, (p. 11), "It is the very nature of life to strive to continue in being. Since this continuance can be secured only by constant renewals, life is a self-renewing process. What nutrition and reproduction are to physiological life, education is to social life." My purpose is, however, to point out the dangers of the organic metaphor, not to criticize Dewey's use of it in the chapter cited. (Passage cited with permission of the Macmillan Company.)

the environing culture. There is real point in so doing in a variety of contexts. If we consider, in particular, anthropological or historical studies in which specific cultures are sometimes taken as units of investigation with a view toward determining their internal structures or the laws governing their structural changes, it may be desirable to group acculturating processes under a single rubric and to study their place in the "patterns of culture" as well as their mechanisms. In psychological investigations, too, where the attempt is made to discover cross-cultural laws of learning, it may be convenient to classify all processes of social learning under a single label as preliminary to this attempt. The organic metaphor in these contexts is perhaps helpful in comparing acculturating processes to regenerative processes in the biological organism. Like the latter, acculturating processes may be studied as relating to other phenomena, and as comprising a variety of mechanisms, whose laws need to be determined.

Nevertheless, when the organic metaphor is transplanted into practical contexts in which social policy is at stake, it may become positively misleading, since it makes no room for distinctions that are of the highest importance in practical issues. There are, for example, no moral distinctions among regenerative processes in the individual organism, whereas such distinctions, with respect to cultural "regenerative" processes, are often at the very center of social controversy. Such distinctions are expressed, for example, in the separation of teaching from force, propaganda, threat, and indoctrination. In addition, biological regenerative processes are not, in general, considered subject to choice and control, whereas social processes, to a significant extent, are, and it is, moreover, just where alternative choices are thought to be possible that issues of social policy take shape.

To compare the continuity of cultures to that of individual lives is, moreover to oversimplify in the extreme. For individual continuity, there are fairly definite biological criteria and the range of variation consonant with continuity is fairly well given, for example, in descriptions of the life cycle. For cultures there are no similarly definite criteria, no known laws of growth or normal patterns of life cycle. We cannot readily say, in advance, how far a culture may change from its past character without losing its identity. Without specification of some standard of cultural continuity, it is thus not clear how education is construed when explained in terms of its contribution to such continuity. The continuity of any culture may be furthered in different, and conflicting ways, in accord with different standards of continuity that may be chosen. It is such differences between standards that are of moral, hence practical significance, though all such standards are compatible with talk of cultural continuity in the abstract.

When, further, the notion of 'function' is transferred from biological to social contexts, an analogous indeterminacy results,[26] so that even with some specification of the respect in which cultural continuity is to be understood, to say that the function of education is to preserve cultural continuity still is inadequate. When we speak of the function of this or that biological mechanism, we speak, roughly, of its contribution to the normal or satisfactory working of the organism. For example, to say that the function of the heart-beat is to circulate blood round the body is to say that such blood circulation, which the heart-beat effects in usual circumstances, is indispensable to the normal working of the organism in question. Thus, also, to speak of the function of regenerative processes as the replacement of old cells with new ones is to say that the replacement resulting from the usual operation of such processes is indispensable to the normal working of the biological organism. In such cases, the concept of 'normal working' is fairly clear.

If, however, we are to suppose that the cultural continuity allegedly effected by education is, similarly, indispensable to the normal or satisfactory working of the culture, we require, similarly, a clear notion of such working. Unfortunately such a clear notion is lacking. Thus, waiving, for the moment, all questions concerning the interpretation of 'continuity,' we still cannot claim that assertions about the function of education are clear in the sense in which 'function' statements are clear in biology. We need, at the very least, to provide some independent specification of the standard of normal working that is being assumed.

26. For a detailed analysis, to which my treatment is indebted, see Hempel, C. G.: The logic of functional analysis, in Gross, L.: *Symposium on Sociological Theory*. Evanston, Illinois, Row Peterson and Company, 1959. The heart-beat example in the text is due to Hempel.

Suppose, however, that such specification is supplied in a particular discourse that also specifies a special use of the term 'continuity.' In such a case, the assertion that the function of education is to preserve cultural continuity becomes analogous to biological 'function' statements in point of clarity. Nevertheless, the moral distinctions that are uppermost in issues of educational and social policy contexts are omitted from the picture. What is worse, the positive moral connotation of the term 'function' (which derives, perhaps, from its relation to biologically satisfactory working which is generally favored) suggests that the notion of social function also implies moral value.

It is obvious upon reflection, though, that no moral conclusions can be drawn from attributions of social function in the manner described, and *a fortiori*, that positive evaluation is not implied. Suppose, for example, we specify, first, that by 'continuity' we shall refer to the maintenance of continued attitudes of political and intellectual docility on the part of the population and second, that by 'normal working' we shall refer to the unopposed rule of the current masters of a given dictatorship. We may now group together under the label 'education' all those processes of suppression, deception, distortion, indoctrination and threat by which political and intellectual docility is achieved and we may conclude by declaring that the function of education in the society in question is to preserve its continuity. Given the two specifications mentioned, the assertion is clear and, moreover, true. For the docility resulting from the processes referred to is indeed indispensable to the tranquility of a dictatorship. It does not follow that such processes *ought* to be employed or approved. It does not follow, either, that dictatorships *ought* to work normally or satisfactorily in the specified sense, i.e., that they ought to be unopposed. The moral issues are not only not stressed in social 'function' statements, but are often confused by the socially irrelevant connotation of value surrounding the term 'function.'

In the example just discussed, it is clear that a moralist might quarrel with the specification given of 'normal working'; he might also propose a different use for 'continuity.' In this way, he might be able to retain the assertion that the function of education is to preserve continuity, but in a wholly different interpretation. Alternatively, he might abandon the 'function' assertion to others, expressing his moral views instead by saying that the teacher has obligations that are independent of social continuity in various prevalent senses, namely, obligations to tell the truth, to respect the intelligence of the student, to earn his trust by being sincere and open in his dealings with him.

We may approach the general point we have here been emphasizing by a consideration of the notion of teaching, which is considerably narrower than that of acculturation. Every culture, we may say, normally gets newborn members to behave according to its norms, however these are specified, and many cultures have agencies devoted to this job. But not every way of getting someone to behave according to some norm is teaching. Some such ways are purely informal and indirect, operating largely by association and contact, as languages are normally learned. But not every formal and deliberate way is teaching, either. Behavior may be effectively brought into accord with norms through threats, hypnosis, bribery, drugs, lies, suggestion, and open force. Teaching may, to be sure, proceed by various methods, but some ways of getting people to do things are excluded from the standard range of the term 'teaching.' To teach, in the standard sense, is at some points at least to submit oneself to the understanding and independent judgment of the pupil, to his demand for reasons, to his sense of what constitutes an adequate explanation. To teach someone that such and such is the case is not merely to try to get him to believe it: deception, for example, is not a method or a mode of teaching. Teaching involves further that, if we try to get the student to believe that such and such is the case, we try also to get him to believe it for reasons that, within the limits of his capacity to grasp, are *our* reasons. Teaching, in this way, requires us to reveal our reasons to the student and, by so doing, to submit them to his evaluation and criticism.

To teach someone, not that such and such is the case, but rather *how* to do something, normally involves showing him how (by description or example) and not merely setting up conditions under which he will, in fact, be likely to learn how. To throw a child into the river is not, in itself, to teach him how to swim; to send one's daughter to dancing school is not, in itself, to teach her how to dance. Even to teach someone *to* do something (rather than how to do it) is not simply to try to get him to do it; it is also to make accessible to him, at some stage, our reasons and purposes in getting him to do it. To teach is thus, in the standard use of the term, to acknowledge the "reason" of the pupil, i.e. his demand for and judgment of reasons, even though such demands are not uniformly appropriate at every phase of the teaching interval.

The distinctions here discussed between teaching and fostering the acquisition of modes of behavior or belief are, we may say, distinctions of *manner*. They depend on the manner in which such acquisition is fostered. The organic metaphor, as we have seen, focuses on the continuity of the culture's life,—in effect, on the behavioral norms and beliefs forming the *content* of the culture. It makes no distinctions in manner of acquisition of this content, of the sort we have illustrated by referring to the concept of 'teaching.' It is these distinctions, however, that are central to moral issues concerning social and educational policy. The usefulness of the organic metaphor in certain contexts cannot be taken to show that the distinctions of manner referred to are of no practical or moral moment, that, for example, teachers ought, by any means and above all, to adjust students to the prevailing culture (specified in any way you like) and to ensure its continuity (no matter how specified). Whether teachers ought or ought not to do just that or some alternative is an independent and serious moral question that requires explicit attention. That it receives no emphasis in the organic metaphor indicates not that the question is unimportant, but that this metaphor is inappropriate in practical contexts.

We shall end this discussion by trying to show how fundamental the question of manner is, and we shall refer here again to the concept of 'teaching.' We have already taken pains to indicate that the notion of teaching is considerably narrower than that of acculturation. The fact that every culture may be said to renew itself by getting newborn members to behave according to its norms emphatically does not mean that such renewal is everywhere a product of teaching in the standard sense we have discussed. To favor the widest diffusion of teaching as a mode and as a model of cultural renewal is, in fact, a significant social option of a fundamental kind, involving the widest possible extension of reasoned criticism to the culture itself.

That this option may, in particular societies, lead to great changes in fundamental norms, beliefs, and social institutions, with respect to the prevailing culture, is indeed possible, even highly likely. But such a consequence need not always follow. In particular, it is not likely to follow where the culture itself institutionalizes reasoned procedures in its basic spheres, where it welcomes the exercise of criticism and judgment, where, that is to say, it is democratic culture in the strongest sense. To support the widest diffusion of teaching as a model of cultural renewal is, in effect, to support something peculiarly consonant with the democratization of culture and something that poses a threat to cultures whose basic social norms are institutionally protected from criticism. Such support is thus consistent with the vision of a culture where understanding is not limited and where critical judgment of policy is not the institutionalized privilege of one class, where policy change is not perforce arbitrary and violent, but channelled through institutions operating by reasoned persuasion and freely given consent. Many, even most, social thinkers have shrunk before such a vision and argued that culture cannot long survive under democracy in this sense. Others have urged the fullest institutionalization of reasoned criticism, fully aware that such a course indeed threatens societies with rigid power divisions, but denying that all societies are therefore threatened and that *no* culture can survive which rests on free criticism freely interchanged. The issue, in short, is not whether culture shall be renewed, but in what *manner* such renewal is to be institutionalized. It is this fundamental practical issue that must not be obscured in practical contexts by metaphors appropriate elsewhere.

## Chapter IV

# TEACHING

W E HAVE, in the last chapter, indicated how the notion 'teaching' suggests a crucial distinction with regard to the manner in which learning may proceed. What was involved in this phase of our discussion was, of course, the everyday, standard use of 'teaching,' and not some stipulated use. This standard use deserves further, detailed attention, for the word figures centrally in numerous discussions of education where the context makes plain that it is to be taken in the ordinary way. We turn then, in the present chapter, to an examination of the term 'teaching,' in an effort to understand the ways in which it is typically applied, and that to which it typically refers. Our concern, like that of descriptive definition, discussed in Chapter 1, is thus to provide an account of the accepted meaning of the notion 'teaching.' We shall not, however, attempt to provide here an explicit definition, but only an informal discussion of certain elements of this accepted meaning.

We may begin by recalling the difference, noted above in Chapter 2, between "success" and "intentional" uses of the verb 'to teach.' In the "success" use, a word refers to more than just the doing of something; it refers also to the successful outcome of what one is doing or has done. To have built a house is more than to have been occupied in building activity; it is also to have gained success in this activity. So, to have taught someone how to swim is more than to have been occupied in teaching someone to swim; it is also to have succeeded.

Let us now, for the sake of simplifying the process of our analysis, abstract from considerations relating to success, and restrict our inquiry to "intentional" uses of the verb. With such a restriction understood, we may classify the teaching referred to by the verb as an activity: it is something that one normally engages in or is occupied in doing. Jones may be engaged in teaching Smith how to operate an electric saw, just as he may be engaged in painting his house. Indeed, to say of Jones that he is teaching is normally to convey that he is engaged in teaching.[27] Teaching is, further, directed toward a certain result: it is a goal-oriented activity.

It is worth noting that not everything true of Jones and expressible by a verb form can be so described. Jones is not normally said to be engaged in breathing, sitting, or strolling, though he breathes, sits, and strolls. Though he owns property, he is not said to be engaged in owning property; although he has reached the age of 57, he is not ordinarily described as having been occupied in reaching the age of 57. Teaching is engaged in, it is directed toward a goal the attainment of which normally involves attention and effort, and provides a relevant definition of success. Breathing, sitting and strolling are not oriented toward goals in specifiable ways; we do not speak of success in breathing, sitting, or strolling. To own property and to reach the age of 57 do not embody strivings for certain goals; they are not even described as things being done. "What is he doing?" may be answered by "He is sitting," ". . . is strolling," ". . . is hunting," ". . . is teaching," but not by "He is owning property," " . . . is reaching the age of 57." In the latter cases, indeed, the present participle is normally inapplicable alto-

27. This matter of what is normally conveyed or understood by a statement concerns something weaker than what is implied by the statement. Nowell-Smith has discussed such a notion under the label of 'contextual implication.' (See Nowell-Smith, P. H.: *Ethics.* London, Penguin Books, Ltd., 1954, p. 80.) He writes, "I shall say that a statement *p* contextually implies a statement *q* if anyone who knew the normal conventions of the language would be entitled to infer *q* from *p in the context in which they occur."* He also stresses that contextual implications may be expressly withdrawn, but that unless they are withdrawn, we are entitled to presume that the inference holds in the context in question. The notion of what is normally conveyed though not implied by a given statement need not, of course, be interpreted just in the way Nowell-Smith interprets it; the present text uses the notion but is neutral with respect to variant explanations of it. For other recent analyses of teaching, see Smith, B. O.: On the anatomy of teaching, *Journal of Teacher Education,* 7:339 (December) 1956, and A concept of teaching, *Teachers College Record,* 61:229 (February) 1960.

gether. We may say "He owns," but not "He is owning"; we may say "He has reached the age of 57," but not " . . . is reaching the age of 57."

By contrast, if Jones is working on a puzzle, he is trying to solve it; if he is said to be painting his house, he is normally understood to be trying to get it painted; if he is described as teaching Smith how to operate an electric saw, he is normally taken to be trying to get Smith to learn its operation. What he is doing is thus tied to a goal striven for, which may or may not in fact be attained. Jones' working on the puzzle may be fruitless; it may be too hard for him. He may succeed and, moreover, do a fine job in painting his house and he may, furthermore, be successful in teaching Smith how to work the saw. In each case, the activity engaged in is oriented toward some goal defining its success and normally requiring extended effort for its attainment. In each case, too, such attainment provides one index of proficiency.

Now one may, of course, try to do many things, not all which are themselves activities which involve further tryings. One may, for example, try to sit (on a particular chair), or try to breathe (in a room with little oxygen or with an injured lung) or try to stroll (but be interrupted by unexpected guests). Such tryings are themselves oriented toward goals and may or may not be successful. It does not follow that sitting, breathing and strolling are species of trying or involve trying generally. One cannot try to sit without trying but we often sit without trying.

It is, furthermore, true that on particular occasions sitting itself, for example, may be associated *in some way* with trying. A man may be sitting in an effort to relax and catch his breath, knowing that too much exercise is bad for his heart. Nevertheless, people often do sit without trying thereby to relax or to do anything at all. To describe someone as sitting is not, in itself, to convey that he is trying to accomplish something in particular. By contrast, to describe someone as working on a puzzle is to convey that he is trying to solve it, to describe someone as painting his house is normally to convey that he is trying to get it painted, to say of someone that he is teaching a pupil how to work an electric saw is ordinarily to convey that he is trying to get to get him to learn how to work it.

One misunderstanding must here be forestalled. To work on a puzzle all afternoon is not, in every case, to try to solve it during the afternoon. The puzzle may be a very difficult one and known to be difficult, and the man working on it may have no hope of solving it in a few hours; he may in fact not be trying to solve it in a few hours. But he cannot be said to have been working on it even during the afternoon unless what he was doing was done in an effort to solve it, with or without some special time restriction. Similarly, one may be painting one's house all day without trying to get it painted by nightfall. But if one were not trying to get it painted at all, ever, one could hardly be said, without considerable qualification, to have spent the day painting one's house. Finally, learning to operate an electric saw may in fact require many lessons. Jones may thus be teaching Smith for an hour or two without trying to get him to learn the operation of the saw in an hour or two. But, unless what Jones does is done in the attempt to get Smith to learn its operation, he cannot well be said, in normal circumstances, to be teaching him how to operate an electric saw. The goal of an activity, in sum, may lie beyond the boundaries of the activity or some segment of it or may lack temporal conditions altogether; nevertheless, engaging in the activity involves trying, generally.

Finally, it should be noted that teaching has here been said normally to involve an effort to achieve learning, but the converse is, as a matter of fact, false. Efforts to achieve learning cannot generally be said to involve teaching, as we have emphasized in the discussion of manner in the previous chapter. Thus, though the achievement of learning is indispensable to teaching success, it is not in itself sufficient; the learning must, in addition, be accomplished in the appropriate manner.

That teaching, as normally understood, is an activity, requiring effort and allowing for the exercise and development of proficiency, and oriented toward a goal that may lie beyond any segment of it, we have already seen. We must now try to make clearer its temporal characteristics. As an activity, teaching takes time. Suppose I told you I had been teaching John, and you asked, "When?" If I said, "Yesterday, at exactly 3:15 p.m., but neither before nor after," this answer would be thought absurd. Teaching is no instantaneous occurrence, like a thunderbolt or the flash of a falling star across the sky. Thus the question, "At exactly what moment were you engaged in teaching John?" makes no obvious sense, while "For how long were you busy teaching John?" is a perfectly legitimate question.[28]

It should now be noted that the question, "For how long have you been teaching John?" may receive, roughly, two sorts of answers. One answer may refer to relatively short intervals, for example "two hours." Another answer may refer to longer intervals, for example, "Three weeks," or "Two and a half years." Let us call all such intervals 'teaching-intervals' and notice that not every part of every teaching-interval is also a teaching-interval. If Jones has been teaching Smith how to drive an automobile, for the last three weeks, he has still, surely, not been teaching him, even during these last three weeks, while Smith has been having his lunch, during his working hours, or while he has been asleep or visiting friends. Rather, this three week interval is characterized by a certain pattern of relatively unitary teaching-intervals, which we may here call 'lessons.'

If a continuous teaching-interval is one all of whose interval parts are themselves teaching-intervals of the same sort, then we may here construe a lesson as a continous teaching-interval that is not itself part of some other continuous teaching-interval. A patterned sequence of lessons may then go to make up a complex teaching-interval such as a course of instruction or part of such a course. Though lessons are smaller than courses, every lesson is still an interval and not a moment, despite the fact that such important happenings as a pupil's seeing the point may indeed be momentary events highlighting the lessons during which they occur.

Let us now attend to the single lesson. What characterizes teaching during the lesson? What must we observe in order to decide that what is going on before us is a case of teaching? We have already stressed that teaching is an activity involving the attempt to achieve a certain sort of learning within certain restrictions of manner. But the implications of this point deserve to be spelled out in answer to the questions posed above.

For it is often supposed that activities are all construable as dis-

28. Related questions are discussed in Vendler, Z.: Verbs and times, *The Philosophical Review*, 66:143, (April) 1957.

tinctive patterns of bodily movement. We have already denied that everything expressible in verb forms as a truth about anyone refers to some activity. Surely it takes little further reflection to see that some such descriptions are not readily amenable to analysis into statements about movement. That Jones now owns 740 acres in Texas is completely independent of his present patterns of bodily movement. That he has just turned 45 is equally independent of his present motions, though, presumably, some general connection with his physiological condition may be expected. Such cases are relatively easy to segregate, however, and to label 'states,' in order to succumb to the temptation to maintain that activities, by contrast, *are* all construable as distinctive patterns of bodily movement. For activities, so the argument runs, are after all things we do, and what is doing but effecting some change in the environment by producing some movement?

The latter argument is, indeed, plausible but nevertheless misguided. It is, to begin with, true that the states in question are *not* normally classified as things we do. The question, "What is he doing now?" can hardly be answered by "Owning 740 acres in Texas" or "Just turning 45." It is, further, true that of the things that do answer this question, *some* are readily seen to refer to distinctive patterns of bodily movement. For example, "Just sitting," "Breathing regularly" (said by a nurse of a patient), and "Strolling through the park," are all appropriate answers and indicate some pattern of movement (where this is taken broadly as including posture or orientation as well as motion).

It is, however, also true that other appropriate answers to the question "What is he doing now?" include, for example, "Working on a geometry problem," an activity-description which turns out quite resistant to the attempt to interpret it as referring to some distinctive pattern of movements, as we shall try to show in a moment. The point to see now is that 'doing' is a broad category including things that *prima facie*, at least, are construable as movement patterns as well as things that are not. It is this fact that undermines the argument that activities must be patterns of movement since they are things we do.

But this fact must be examined concretely by reference to examples. Let us compare the case of breathing with that of working on a geometry problem, both admittedly doings, in contrast to what were above called 'states.' How is it possible to tell that a person is breathing during a given interval? We observe a certain repetitive pattern of movement associated with the sequence of air intake and expulsion during the interval. Compare the case of a boy working on a geometry problem during a given interval. He must, of course, be doing something reasonable with the aim of solving the problem. To be working on it, he must be trying as well as doing. What is observably done may, furthermore, vary with the situation, and will be associated with reflection in any event. To know that the boy before us is really working on a geometry problem and not simply playing with the paper, we need to judge that he is in fact thinking but, furthermore, we need to judge that whatever he is doing involves the hope of solving a problem. To judge that he is thinking is already to go beyond his manifest bodily movements (though not perhaps beyond certain unobserved internal changes). To judge what he is trying to do, moreover, we should ordinarily have to go beyond his bodily movements during the present interval. We may, for example, know that he is enrolled in a geometry course at school, that he has been assigned the problem as homework, that the solution is to be handed in the next day, that he has always turned in his homework promptly in the past, that he has frequently expressed the desire to major in mathematics.

All these external items of information are clues to his present intent, in the light of which we interpret what he is doing (including his present movements) as "Working on the problem." His observable motions might be any of an indefinite number. He may pace the floor, stare out the window, look at a diagram, turn the paper sideways, frown, etc. Each of these motions is, furthermore, frequently duplicated in cases having nothing to do with working on a geometry problem. None is thus either a necessary or a sufficient condition of such working. (It follows that all taken together cannot be necessary and that all taken alternatively cannot be sufficient.) Here, then, is a case of an activity that is not identifiable with some distinctive pattern of movements despite the fact that it is a "doing," something done. Aside from the fact that thinking is involved, the doing of the interval requires interpretation in terms of its environing context.

Returning now to the previous questions concerning teaching during the single lesson, it seems obvious that the case is parallel to that of working on a geometry problem during a given interval. Teaching, too, involves trying as well as doing—trying to get someone to learn something. Here too, what is observably done in the way of patterns of movement varies indefinitely and is duplicated in contexts where no teaching is involved at all. The teacher may talk or he may be silent, he may write or he may not, he may ask questions or not, he may use special materials or equipment or he may not. Anything of this sort, furthermore, may be done by people not engaged in teaching. Whether a man is teaching or just criticizing, meditating, arguing, sulking, entertaining etc., is thus not something that can be read off directly from the movements of the teacher during the lesson. Aside from the question of ascertaining the teacher's thinking, the interpretation of what is done during the lesson depends on the intent with which it is done and the determination of such intent varies with information about the lesson's context. Teaching cannot thus be construed as some distinctive pattern of movements executed by the teacher.

In the light of this analysis, it appears that attempts to think of teaching in extreme behavioristic terms are, at best, ambiguous and, at worst, totally misguided. Returning to the geometry example, it may plausibly be argued that the boy has, in fact, not solved the problem unless he can produce a proof in stated or written form. Proofs can be checked for validity, once produced. In this weak sense, it may be admitted that "behavioristic" evidence (with respect to the stated or written product of the boy's motions) enters into our judgment as to the success of his activity. It does not follow that the *production* of proofs can be generally characterized in advance, that we can say generally what pattern of speaking or writing movements constitutes a sufficient condition for problem-solution in geometry or mathematics. That such a characterization is impossible is demonstrable on mathematical grounds alone. This situation is general in science as well, where, though theories, once produced, may be evaluated as to their scientific worth, we have no general rules for the production of worthwhile theories. To think of problem-solving as a complex sequence of movements governed by rule is thus a myth.

It surely does not follow that the boy's mere working on the problem (as distinct from his solving it) can be construed as such a sequence. It is mistaken to suppose that learning geometry is a matter of mastering some distinctive pattern of movements, or that teaching geometry consists in prescribing the movements to be made.

Analogously, that a given instance of teaching activity has been successful in achieving learning may plausibly be argued to admit of behaviorial test in the form of some standard examination of pupils' knowledge, skills, or attitudes. It does not follow that teaching may be described as a standard pattern of movements even where it is successful, let alone where it is not. It is thus mistaken to think that one may learn to teach by mastering some distinctive pattern of movements, or that we can teach people to teach by prescribing such a pattern for them, formulated in general rules. What can reasonably be done in the way of teaching people to teach presents, indeed, a crucial problem. Suffice it for the present to remark that whatever rules can profitably be applied here are likely to be comparable to rules profitably used in the teaching of geometry or science rather than to rules of spelling.

To conclude this phase of our discussion, if we are to decide whether or not Jones is engaged in teaching activity during a specified interval, we can neither rely merely on one momentary observation, nor can we rely merely on observations of Jones' movements during the interval in question. Rather, in the light of information that normally goes beyond the interval in question, we have to see whether what Jones is doing is aimed at getting someone to learn something, whether it is not unreasonably thought to be likely to achieve the learning aimed at, and whether it falls within the restrictions of manner peculiar to teaching as ordinarily understood,— in particular, whether acknowledgment of the alleged pupil's judgment is made, whether, e.g. the pupil is not systematically precluded from asking 'How?' 'Why?' or 'On what grounds?'

If Jones is engaged in teaching, he is, then, trying. It is clear that to be trying to do something is not always to succeed. Whether success is also attained depends on factors outside of one's trying: the universe must co-operate. To hunt lions is to try to bag a lion, whereas to bag one is also to succeed in this attempt, and depends on more than just the trying. Succeeding or being successful is not an activity by our earlier standard; it is not something that one engages in, not even something one does. No one engages in being successful, as distinct from trying to appear successful or, in fact, to be successful. Nor, in answer to the question, "What are you doing?" is it thus ever appropriate to say, 'I am being successful in hunting a lion,' though it is surely alright to reply, 'I am hunting a lion.'

To this it might fairly be objected that though the former reply (which refers explicitly to success) is indeed inappropriate, another reply, making indirect reference to success, is not: We can say, in answering a request to tell what someone is doing, 'He's away bagging lions.' It is surely appropriate to say that Jones (off on a hunting expedition) is engaged in bagging lions.

This objection wrongly assumes, however, that there is, in these instances, a tacit reference to success. The verb 'bag' has "success" uses, to be sure, but it also has "intentional" uses, in which it does not imply success. To see that the present illustrative statements are all cases of "intentional" use, we have only to reflect that they are not incompatible with failure. Failure to bag a lion does not falsify the earlier description of our hunter as bagging or as engaged in bagging lions; this description was thus no prediction that at least one lion would, in fact, be bagged. The case is different where a hunter returns claiming to have bagged a lion; here his claim is clearly incompatible with his returning empty-handed. He must not merely have tried to bag a lion; he must have been successful, if he is telling the truth. Our earlier conclusion that success is neither a form of activity nor a species of doing thus stands. Success is, rather, as Ryle has stressed, an appropriate upshot of activities.[29]

That there is an appropriate upshot of an activity means that failure is possible. To try is thus to risk failure. Rules appropriate to a given activity tell us how we ought to conduct our trying to avoid failure, what we ought to do to maximize the likelihood of success. But such rules are not all of the same sort. In certain cases, helpful rules are formulable which, if they are followed, guarantee success; failure in the activity, taken as a whole, is still

29. Ryle, G.: *The Concept of Mind*, Op. cit.

possible, but it never occurs where the rules are followed. Let us call rules guaranteeing success 'exhaustive rules' of an activity. To illustrate, consider a child trying to spell 'cat' correctly, in writing. We might, in this case, formulate helpful exhaustive rules as follows: "First, (leaving a letter-wide space to the left) write 'C'; next, leaving no letter-wide space, write 'A' to the right of 'C,' on the same line; next, leaving no letter-wide space, write 'T' to the right of 'A,' on the same line" (leaving a letter-wide space to the right of 'T'). The child may not, in fact, follow these rules, but they are exhaustive relative to the activity and the context in question since no child who follows them fails in the attempt to spell 'cat' correctly in writing. They are, further, helpful since a child ignorant of the correct spelling of 'cat' may yet know perfectly well how to do what the rules demand of him.

Other rules are 'inexhaustive,' by contrast. Rules for lion-hunting (we may imagine) tell hunters what they ought to do in trying to bag lions. Such rules cover the details of training, preparation, and the conduct of the hunt. One component set of such rules relating to the hunt may be supposed to be: "Aim your loaded gun at the lion; then, when the range and other conditions are right, pull the trigger." Let us assume that the hunter's knowledge and skill are excellent, that he interprets the rightness of conditions correctly, and that he follows this component set of rules as well as the other components, to the letter. It is still not guaranteed that some lion will be bagged; the lion may bound away at exactly the crucial moment. Rules to follow in trying to win games are, similarly, inexhaustive; one may follow all the rules of training and playing and still end by losing the game.

Rules for searching for needles in haystacks are, similarly inexhaustive if they are meant to be helpful, and, as we have suggested earlier, rules for finding geometrical proofs are analogously inexhaustive, though the "computation" rules of elementary arithmetic (say, for doing sums) taught in schools resemble more closely rules of spelling. (It is worth noting the important fact that mathematical rules are not all of one type.)

It is always, to be sure, easy to formulate exhaustive rules that will not be helpful. To the lion-hunting rules already mentioned, we may, for example, add "Kill the lion." Anyone following the latter rule cannot fail to bag a lion, but it is ordinarily true that if he does not know how to bag a lion, neither does he know how to follow the rule. On the other hand, omitting this unhelpful rule has the effect of leaving the whole set inexhaustive. Similarly, to someone seeking advice on how to win a race we might say, "Arrive at the tape before any of the other runners," and to someone searching for a needle in a haystack we might say, "Locate the needle, then bend down and pick it up." Such rules are obviously of no help whatever in normal situations. Unfortunately, it is not as *obviously* unhelpful, though in fact equally so, to tell geometry students seeking a proof, "Find some ordered sequence of statements ending with the theorem in question, and such that each statement in the sequence is either an axiom or logically derivable from its predecessors in the sequence." The problem facing these students is just exactly how to go about finding such a sequence, and no rules that are helpful in this regard are at the same time capable of guaranteeing success. Analogous considerations are applicable to the search for fruitful scientific theories, as suggested earlier.

If we turn now to the case of teaching, it appears that it is more analogous to lion-hunting than to spelling, with respect to rules. No rules designed to improve the likelihood of success are both exhaustive and helpful to the would-be teacher, at least so far as we can tell. Rules of teaching may at best improve teaching, in the sense of rendering it more effective; they cannot exhaustively rule out failure. We may, if we like, call teaching a 'practical art' in that it is (speaking broadly) an activity, aimed at a goal that defines success, and improvable by rules that do not, however, guarantee success. The provision of such rules is one outstanding job of educational research. Some such rules will exclude ineffective sorts of trying to accomplish success in teaching, others will indicate which among the effective sorts are relatively more effective than others.

As a practical art, teaching resembles medicine, engineering, and cooking, for instance. These arts are all, furthermore, distinguished from science, taken as a body of statements purporting to be true, on the best available evidence. Of such statements, it makes sense to say that they are true or false, well or ill confirmed, believed or disbelieved. None of these descriptions applies to teaching, bridge-building, baking, or the care of patients. The latter are activities, not statements. Conversely, statements are not done or engaged in. When the term 'science' denotes a set of statements, it is thus to be distinguished from terms denoting activities. Nevertheless, scientific statements do not just happen or grow of themselves. They are themselves products of the scientist's activity, for which we may employ the term 'scientific inquiry.' Such inquiry is itself another of the practical arts, like teaching and bridge-building. It, too, is something engaged in, aimed at the development of adequate theories, improvable by rules that cannot, however, guarantee its success. Scientific inquiry is, in these respects, on a par with all the other practical arts.

There is, however, another respect in which it is central to all the rest. The results at which it aims are statements adequate to all available factual evidence. It is just such statements that are used not only for inferences and predictions but for the construction of rules of activity, rules thus appropriate to all the practical arts, including inquiry itself. These statements provide information concerning the relative effectiveness of procedures undertaken to achieve given results, and they indicate also which procedures are worthless. They tell us, in detail, of the ways in which procedures may conflict with each other, and of the consequences they may have which fall outside the range of desired results. All such information is clearly relevant to enhancing the effectiveness of activities generally. Scientific inquiry into education, (or educational research) to take a particular example, may yield statements indicating what teaching procedures are most effective, what combinations of procedures are in conflict, what side-effects of given procedures may be expected. The relation of educational research to teaching may thus be compared with the relation of physical research to engineering, or, better, with the relation of medical research to the clinical practice of medicine.

The last example serves indeed as a reminder that the relation between practical art and what may be called its 'underlying science' must not be oversimplified. In particular, it must not be supposed that to each practical art (however the members of this vague category are specified) there corresponds some unique underlying science. Medical research is not limited to biology and neither is educational research restricted to psychology. The divisions of the sciences are, to be sure, not in themselves very important or very constant, but whatever reality they may have at any time derives largely from the autonomous development of scientific theory, independently of the aims defining the practical arts. Increasingly, psychology is thought relevant to medicine, biology and chemistry to psychiatry, physics to government. Educational research must not be conceived as a single science, but rather as the common focus of many sciences with bearings on educational practice. These sciences include not only psychology, but also, for example, sociology, anthropology, biology and economics.

Though no *unique* science underlies each of the major practical arts, the degree to which *some* body of theoretical science underlies an art is an important factor determining its degree of professionalization. For the rules that guide practice may embody factual information without resulting in every case from scientific inquiry of a sophisticated sort. They may belong to the heritage of common sense, or folklore, or the accumulated experience of practitioners. Such rules are, often, quite reliable but they are isolated in the sense that they are not clearly related to some theoretical structure of scientific statements. They are, thus, practically helpful to the practitioner but they do not enable him to understand or explain, in any general sense, what he is doing or why it is that his procedures work.[30]

Compare the knowledge of the effectiveness of various herbs that guided medical practice in earlier days with the theoretical knowledge guiding the most enlightened medical practice today. The former was isolated, providing no general understanding of recommended procedures. (This is not to say that such procedures were ineffective; in many cases they anticipated later, enlightened procedures.) Medical practice, in great part, derives its present professional status from its relationship to bodies of scientific theory which progressively enable the physician to understand and explain what he is doing. Such ability means that the physician is not merely following rules of thumb but is exercising practical judgment and discretion in choosing and varying the treatment of indi-

30. For a treatment of related issues, see O'Connor, D. J.: *An Introduction to the Philosophy of Education.* New York, Philosophical Library, 1957, Chapter 5.

vidual cases in the light of his theoretical equipment.

The question of professional status is, however, a question of degree and is subject to great changes in the course of time. We have already compared the primitive knowledge of herbs with contemporary medical research. Few arts can, in fact, now rival medicine in point of professional status. At the other extreme, we may consider cooking, which is still largely a matter of following rules of thumb, accumulated by trial and error and (except for the greatly increased rôle of cookbooks) passed on from mother to daughter, from friend to friend, and from master chef to apprentice, with little or no theoretical understanding of why the recommended procedures are effective or why they are thought preferable to others.

There is, of course, no precisely defined continuum here, nor any accurate way of placing other activities on even our rough hypothetical continuum, ranging from medicine to cooking. Many observers, forced to hazard a guess concerning the position of teaching, would place it in the middle, somewhat closer to the side of cooking. This assignment, if correct, is however, a matter that is subject to change, and there is no *a priori* reason why the practice of teachers should not increasingly be guided by theoretical bodies of scientific information. In part, such progress depends on the independent development of, in particular, the social sciences. In part, too, it depends on continued willingness to apply scientific inquiry to educational practice. In any event, the increasing professionalization of teaching is, in good part, dependent on such a development, which would enable the teacher more and more to judge and choose procedures on the basis of theoretical understanding, rather than their mere conformity to cookbook specifications embodied in the lore transmitted by previous generations. This is, again, not to say that such lore is ineffective in fact, nor that it should not presently be followed. On the contrary, we have, at present, little better to rely on in whole ranges of education. It is, nevertheless, possible to hold a dual attitude toward such lore: to be prepared to follow its direction in current practice while, at the same time, encouraging the growth of scientific inquiry into teaching and its increasing use in the criticism and revision of our whole educational heritage.

It is important, in concluding the present discussion, to strive for a general view of the relation between teaching and scientific inquiry in the light of our preceding analysis. They are two different activities or practical arts, controlled by different goals. The results of inquiry may be used in improving the practice of teaching, but the goals of inquiry are nevertheless distinct from the goals of teaching. The aim of inquiry is to construct theories adequate to all the facts, theories that may thus be taken as our best estimates of the truths of nature and as guides to action. In the course of working toward this aim, inquiry normally ranges far from the practical, everyday world to which its results may one day be applied. It is because of this abstraction from the practical world that scientific inquiry is able to provide compact and comprehensive principles explaining what goes on in that world.

The goals of inquiry thus lead it to diverge from the sphere of other practical arts whose concerns center in the world of everyday action. Teachers, for example, aim at the achievement of certain sorts of learning in their pupils here and now, not at the development of a theoretical apparatus for explaining such learning. The divergence in question is understandable and legitimate in view of the different goals that are operative. What is perhaps more important to note, however, is that the improvement of practice is not facilitated but retarded by attempts to close the gap. The more inquiry is restricted to local and practical spheres, the less capable it is of attaining general, theoretical grasp, and hence of guiding and explaining practice.

If inquiry is to be effectively related to the practice of teaching, the divergence of goal between teacher and educational researcher needs to be recognized as legitimate and as calling for different working distances from the world of practice. There needs, of course, also to be a relation of mutual and sympathetic interest between teachers and educational researchers. Teachers must not only understand the researcher's divergence of aim and his difference in practical orientation; they must also be able to comprehend the implications of his results for their own work. For their part, researchers must not only appreciate the goals inspiring teaching; they must also understand its peculiar problems in diverse situations and be willing to take these as starting-points for research and as end-points to which research results may be applied.

*Chapter V*

# TEACHING AND TELLING

THE preceding chapter presented some general considerations relating to teaching as an activity. In the present chapter, the attempt is made to highlight certain detailed features of teaching by an examination of three paradigms representing frequent uses of the verb 'to teach' and by an extended comparison with corresponding uses of 'to tell.' It is hoped that this analysis will not only provide a fuller view of what is referred to by the familiar word 'teach' but that it will be of some practical help as well, in clarifying discussions concerned with the curriculum.

Let us begin by introducing three pairs of schemata, each pair comprised by a schema paradigmatic of some use of 'to teach,' and another schema paradigmatic of a corresponding use of 'to tell.' Each schema will be referred to in the ensuing discussion by means of the letter preceding it.

A. $X$ tells $Y$ that. . . . . . . . . . . .     C. $X$ tells $Y$ to. . . . . . . . . . . .
B. $X$ teaches $Y$ that. . . . . . . . . .     D. $X$ teaches $Y$ to. . . . . . . . .
E. $X$ tells $Y$ how to. . . . . . . . . . . . . . . .
F. $X$ teaches $Y$ how to. . . . . . . . . . . . .

'To tell' is suitable for our projected comparison because, like 'to teach' in flexibility, it can be used in the three ways represented by the three pairs of schemata above, and furthermore, it is closely related in application to 'to teach': much, if not all, teaching involves telling. By contrast, 'to instruct' may be used in contexts of the form '$X$ instructs $Y$ to . . . . .,' parallel to D, but not normally in contexts of the form, '$X$ instructs $Y$ that . . . . .' (parallel to B) nor in contexts of the form, '$X$ instructs $Y$ how to . . . . .' (parallel to F). On the other hand, 'to inform' is normally used in contexts of the form 'X informs Y that . . . . .' but neither in contexts of the form 'X informs Y how to . . . . .' nor in those of the form 'X informs Y to . . . . . ' 'To tell' is thus superior as a standard of comparison.

Let us now compare A (telling that) and B (teaching that). Telling, like teaching, may be said normally to involve trying. But, unlike teaching, it does not generally involve X's trying to get Y to learn. Thus, if X is successful in teaching Y that Columbus discovered America, X learns (at some time) that Columbus discovered America. If X is successful in telling Y that Columbus discovered America, we cannot infer that Y has at any time learned this fact or that he ever will. For X to have been successful in telling Y that Columbus discovered America (for X to have indeed told him) does, to be sure, ordinarily require the fulfillment of certain conditions by the hearer Y. For example, Y must have been awake, within earshot, and capable (at least in some way, e.g , through interpreters) of understanding the language in which X's message was couched. (If Y is unconscious, just out of earshot or incapable of comprehending X's language, we may describe X's energetic efforts at communication as a case of 'trying to tell', or 'telling' in its "intentional" use, but we withhold ascriptions of success.) Nevertheless, success in telling surely does not require that Y learn X's message, now or ever. Y may comprehend it and show no further trace of it. Even if Y was daydreaming or otherwise preoccupied and claims not to have heard X's message, it is not entirely clear that X's telling is therefore unsuccessful: X may reply, "Yes, I told you alright, but you didn't hear—too busy reading the paper to listen." (He would never say, analogously, "Yes, I told you alright, but you were unconscious," or ". . . don't understand English" or ". . . . were too far away to hear me.") In any event, whatever things success in telling does require it is clear that Y's learning is not one of them.

By contrast, for X to have taught Y (been successful in teaching Y) that Columbus discovered America does normally imply that Y has learned that Columbus discovered America. What this learning consists in and how it may be exhibited are important but separate questions. Y must presumably be able to state the fact or else to apply it indirectly, but the exact details are irrelevant for our present purposes. How long must $Y$ retain the fact? This, too, is a question the precise answer to which (if there be such) is independent of present concerns. $Y$ may forget the fact rather soon, but unless he has retained it for some time, $X$ cannot truly be said to have been successful in teaching him that Columbus discovered America. The reference to retention indicates, incidentally, why testing is relevant to teaching but not to telling. If a test of the pupil shows no retention, it may be reasonable to infer (assuming there was no earlier retention now evaporated) that the teaching has not been successful. Under the same circumstances, however, the telling may have been quite successful.

What it means for $Y$ to have learned that Columbus discovered America is, we have said, an important question but one independent of our present concerns. We must, however, not suppose that all statements of B form are alike in the sort of learning that is indispensable to teaching success. Indeed, some such statements deserve separate classification because they are significantly different and crucial in educational discussion and serve, moreover, further to distinguish A from B forms. Let us refer to sentences such as 'Columbus discovered America' as 'fact-stating.' It is now important to recognize that A and B forms may take not only fact-stating sentences in their respective blanks, but also norm-stating sentences, for example, 'One ought to pay one's debts,' or 'Honesty is the best policy.'[31] Thus, we may speak of telling someone that he ought to pay his debts, or of teaching someone that honesty is the best policy. It is statements of the latter sort that we need to examine, after some preliminary remarks.

The distinctions between "facts" and "values" or "norms," and the distinctions between "factual" and "ethical" or "moral" statements have been much discussed by philosophers and acute contri-

31. The category of norm-stating sentences here introduced includes not only those like 'One ought to pay one's debts,' which are usually judged to express moral principles, but also those like 'Honesty is the best policy,' which may rather be judged to express practical maxims, without grounding in moral principles proper. The category of norm-stating sentences is thus considerably wider here than in other interpretations usual in discussions of ethics. The wider interpretation is here adopted as being more suitable to the educational issues that are our main concern.

butions have been made by many recent philosophical analysts. The questions are difficult and complicated and no single resolution has won uniform acceptance, though numerous important points have been brought to light.[32] The present distinction between fact-stating and norm-stating sentences is, however, not intended as a general answer to these questions. Thus, the distinction here suggested leaves it an entirely open question whether norm-stating sentences are "cognitive," "true or false," or "empirically confirmable," and, equally, whether truths are not themselves "normative" in force. Norm-stating sentences throughout the present discussion are, rather, those that lend themselves to a peculiar ambiguity when they are used to fill the blank in contexts of the form '$Y$ has learned that . . . .' What is this ambiguity?

If Jones is said to have learned that honesty is the best policy, we may, ordinarily, interpret what is said in two ways distinguishable, roughly, as follows. We may, on the one hand, suppose that Jones has acquired the norm or pattern of action referred to, that he has developed a tendency to pursue the policy of honesty in his own conduct, that he has learned to behave honestly or to be honest. The acquisition of the norm or pattern of action need not be the whole of Jones' learning, on this interpretation, but it is an indispensable part, so that evidence of Jones' flagrant dishonesty would be considered to refute the assertion that he had learned that honesty is the best policy. Analogously, evidence that a schoolboy had defiantly refused to return the money he admits having borrowed would, on the present interpretation, show that he had not learned that he ought to pay his debts. Let us refer to the foregoing interpretation as 'active.'

We may, on the other hand, have a non-active interpretation of the statements, 'Jones has learned that honesty is the best policy,' or 'Jones has learned that he ought to pay his debts.' On this non-active interpretation, the acquisition by Jones of the patterns of action referred to is not required by the truth of these statements. Thus, evidence that Jones is dishonest would not be supposed to

32. For a critical survey of these questions and recent approaches to them, see Aiken, H.D.: Moral philosophy and education, *Harvard Educational Review.* 25:39, (Winter) 1955, reprinted in Scheffler, I.: *Philosophy and Education,* Op. cit.

refute the first, nor would evidence of wilful non-payment of ac-knowledged debts be taken as refuting the second. Such evidence might, at most, be construed as a sign of Jones' weakness of will, irrationality, or "inconsistency" as between behavior and belief. It would not be thought incompatible with the truth of the statements themselves. In common usage, both active and non-active inter-pretations of our 'learning'-statements are frequent and each is, of course, theoretically legitimate. But these 'learning'-statements are therefore ambiguous and it needs to be made clear which interpre-tation is in fact operative if univocal decisions are to be rendered on important cases to which they refer.

The ambiguity we have just noted, however, results only when *certain* sentences fill the blank in the schema '$Y$ has learned that . . . .' It is these sentences, resulting in the ambiguity mentioned, that we are here calling *norm-stating*, without prejudice as to their cognitive status or lack thereof. All the rest are fact-stating, with-out prejudice as to their normative status or lack thereof.

Let us now examine the result of using a fact-stating sentence to fill the blank in '$Y$ has learned that . . . . .' and see for ourselves a case in which the ambiguity discussed fails to appear. Consider, then, the statement, 'Smith has learned that Columbus discovered America.' In order for the ambiguity in question to appear, both an active and non-active interpretation of this statement must be shown to be applicable. An active interpretation would require that Smith be taken as having acquired the norm or pattern of action referred to by the blank-filling sentence. But no such norm is in fact referred to by this sentence in our present example. Or, putting it in a simpler way, whereas Jones' learning that honesty is the best policy is often taken to imply his learning to be honest and where-as, also, his learning that he ought to pay his debts is often taken to imply his acquiring the tendency to pay his debts, Smith's learning that Columbus discovered America is never taken to imply his learning to be Columbus, or to be America, or to be similar to either, or to acquire the tendency to discover America. The ambi-guity does not arise because the active interpretation cannot here be carried through.

We may now draw various threads together. We have noted that certain sentences (the norm-stating ones) are capable of rendering ambiguous particular 'learning'-contexts in which they are embedded. On the active interpretation of such contexts, the learning to which they refer includes the acquisition of the very norm or pattern of action indicated by the norm-stating sentence. On the non-active interpretation, such acquisition is not an indispensable part of the learning in question. We have, moreover, seen that there are other sentences (the fact-stating ones) for which, since the active interpertation is ruled out for the 'learning'-contexts in which they are embedded, the ambiguity in question fails to appear; the only interpretation appropriate here is non-active in that norm-acquisition is not implied by the 'learning'-statement.

Let us now recall that, in differentiating between A and B, we found success in teaching that . . . . to imply a corresponding learning that . . . , whereas success in telling that . . . . implies nothing of this sort. For statements of A form, it thus makes no difference with respect to conditions of success whether the blank-filling sentences are fact-stating or norm-stating. For the difference between fact-stating and norm-stating sentences is a difference with respect to the sort of *learning* that is described when they are embedded in 'learning that . . . . .'-contexts. Thus, the conditions imposed on $Y$ in order for $X$ to have been successful in telling him that honesty is the best policy are generally identical with those imposed on $Y$ in order for $X$ to have been successful in telling him that Columbus discovered America; for example, $Y$ must have been awake, within earshot, and capable of understanding the language of $X$'s message, etc.

Turning to statements of B form, by contrast, we find that the shift from fact-stating to norm-stating sentences as blank-fillers occasionally does make a difference with respect to the conditions of success of the teaching in question. For such success implies a corresponding learning that . . ., and where the blank-filler here is norm-stating and is given an *active* interpretation in context, the learning in question involves the acquisition by $Y$ of the norm or pattern of action referred to. Success in teaching here comes to imply a sort of norm-acquisition which heretofore, with respect to fact-stating blank-fillers, it did not. Thus, for $X$ to have been successful in teaching $Y$ that honesty is the best policy comes to imply something not implied by $X$'s success in teaching $Y$ that

Columbus discovered America; it comes to imply the acquisition by $Y$ of a norm or pattern of action indicated by the blank-filler. Success in teaching may now be tested by seeing if $Y$'s conduct conforms to the norm in question; failure to conform rules out success.

The difference just pointed out with respect to conditions of teaching success (when the shift is made from fact-stating to norm-stating sentences as blank-fillers of B statements) would be interesting but not nearly so serious as it is, were it not for the ambiguity discussed earlier in connection with norm-stating sentences. For this ambiguity results from the possibility of a non-active as well as an active interpretation of 'learning that . . .'-contexts in which norm-stating sentences are embedded. And when a *non-active* interpretation is given to the learning required by success of the teaching referred to by a given B statement, $Y$'s acquisition of the norm referred to by B's blank-filler is *not* required for teaching success. Such a non-active interpretation in effect assimilates the given B statement to those with fact-stating blank-fillers, where perforce no active interpretation is available. What is most serious, then, in the shift to norm-stating sentences in B contexts is that the B contexts are thereby infected with ambiguity with respect to the teaching success involved. Such ambiguity is of paramount importance for treatments of moral education and the relation between knowledge and conduct,[33] and therefore warrants special attention to B contexts containing norm-stating sentences, and special efforts to resolve the ambiguity in such contexts. What is the danger of this ambiguity?

If the ambiguity is unresolved, a peculiar fallacy is encouraged, with damaging practical as well as theoretical consequences. (Suppose that, where the active interpretation of norm-stating components is adopted we agree to speak, for brevity, of the whole B statement as receiving an active interpretation, in that $Y$'s norm-acquisition is both striven for by $X$, and indispensable to teaching success. Similarly, let us speak of the whole B statement as receiving a non-active interpretation where its norm-stating component is interpreted non-actively as well as in all cases in which its blank-

33. For a discussion of related points see Roland, J.: On "Knowing how" and "Knowing that," *The Philosophical Review*, 67:379, (July) 1958.

filler is fact-stating.) Imagine now that we have, to everyone's satisfaction, established the success of the teaching referred to by a given B statement, with norm-stating component, *in its non-active interpretation*. (We have gathered acknowledged evidence for such success, of the sorts generally presumed adequate for B statements with fact-stating components, that is, we have questioned $Y$ under controlled conditions, presented various statements for him to judge, gotten him to express inferences related to the component in question, and so forth, but failed to examine his conduct with respect to norm-acquisition.) It would be fallacious to infer that we had thereby established the success of our B statement, *in its active interpretation*, that is, that $Y$ had been shown to have acquired the norm referred to by the norm-stating component. The norm may, in fact, have been acquired, but it cannot be assumed to have been acquired on the ground that $Y$ has satisfied a set of criteria for success of a completely different sort.

The fallacy here is facilitated by the ambiguity of B statements and is perhaps one root of the "verbalism" in moral education that believes success in the development of moral character to be the necessary product of success in the (non-active) teaching of ethical formulas. A similar fallacy is encouraged when, in reflecting on his aims in teaching $Y$, $X$ fails to distinguish between trying to bring about $Y$'s acquisition of a certain norm or pattern of conduct and trying to get $Y$ to learn the norm in a manner similar to his learning some historical fact; when, in short, $X$ is not clear as to whether $Y$'s *behaving* contrary to the norm is something that $X$ is trying to eliminate.

The ambiguity under discussion may be related to an ancient problem of philosophy, the question whether virtue can be taught. Socrates is interpreted as having supposed that no one willingly and knowingly chooses to do evil or to reject the good.[34] If someone knows what the good is, he cannot fail to choose it. Thus, virtue can be taught. We need merely to succeed in teaching people to know what is good, and virtuous conduct is guaranteed. In contradistinction to this view, most other philosophers have held that

34. See, for example, Frankena, W.K.: Toward a philosophy of moral education, *Harvard Educational Review.* 28:300, (Fall) 1958, especially section I.

men frequently do reject what they believe to be good and knowingly choose evil. Western religions have, similarly, held that knowledge is not sufficient for virtue, that right will is also required. Man, by virtue of his freedom, may deliberately sin though he knows that the object of his choice is evil. Moral teaching is thus said to be not adequate, since it restricts itself to illuminating the intellect; we need also to strengthen the will and to sensitize the conscience.

In the light of our previous analysis, it would seem that the issue as just stated may not be so fundamental as has been supposed. If we treat 'X teaches Y that honesty is the best policy' on the analogy with 'X teaches Y that Columbus discovered America,' we give it a non-active interpretation, which directs that such teaching be judged successful even in certain cases where Y fails to acquire the norm of honesty in his own conduct. It follows that his acquisition of this norm is independent of the success of the moral teaching to which he has been subjected. This is to say that virtuous conduct is *not* automatically ensured by successful moral teaching.

If, on the other hand, we give an active interpretation to the ambiguous statement 'X teaches Y that honesty is the best policy' (thereby disassociating it from 'X teaches Y that Columbus discovered America'), then the teaching to which it refers cannot be judged successful unless Y acquires the norm of honesty. It follows that if success in moral teaching is attained, the pupil in fact acquires the norm of honesty in his own conduct. This is to say that virtuous conduct *is* automatically ensured by success in moral teaching.

Since, however, the opposition of views, as thus construed, rests on different interpretations of an ambiguous notion, it is mistaken to suppose that they are really in conflict. Each view recognizes the actual cases recognized by the other but describes them differently. To speak a different language, however, is not necessarily to disagree. The crucial case is the one in which the pupil Y demonstrates that he has been successfully taught, in the non-active sense, that honesty is the best policy and yet proceeds to act in ways incompatible with an adoption of the norm of honesty. The views before us do not, however, disagree about this case. Each view makes room for it and allows that it may, in fact, occur. One view will, however, describe it by saying that $Y$ has been successfully taught that honesty is the best policy and yet does not behave in accord with the norm, while the other view will describe it by saying that, although $Y$ admittedly does not behave according to the norm, neither has he been successfully taught it. To put it in more traditional terms, both views allow that intellectual apprehension of moral principles and intellectual avowal of them may go together with a rejection of such principles in conduct, but one view describes such a case as a failure in teaching whereas the other describes it as a failure in will.

If the foregoing analysis is correct, and these views do not really conflict with respect to actual cases, neither is the one superior to the other with respect to these cases. Either one, consistently held, provides a way of describing the facts accurately. The only serious trouble (and it is considerable) arises through shifting from one to the other in midstream. Let us illustrate the consequences of such shifting.

We begin, for example, with the view that acquiring virtuous conduct is indispensable to the success of moral teaching, that is, we decide on active interpretations of all 'teaching that . . .' statements with norm-stating components. Then we decide, in our schools, to teach pupils that honesty is the best policy, i.e., to have them acquire the norm. We may, in consequence, employ methods of exhortation and discussion intended to develop the appropriate norm-governed conduct. Having finished our teaching, we find it a quite difficult matter to decide whether or not we have been successful. For, in order to do that, we should have to determine how pupils are actually behaving generally in situations where the norm of honesty might be presumed to be relevant. We are tempted, in the face of such difficulty, to give up the active interpretation of 'teaching' statements, so that we can assimilate the testing of 'Honesty is the best policy' to that of 'Columbus discovered America' as units of the pupil's learned repertoire. Succumbing to this temptation, we proceed by questioning and other verbal techniques to determine that, on the non-active interpretation of 'teaching,' we have, indeed, been successful. Then, we (more or less unconsciously) shift back to the active interpretation and claim, without further evidence, that we have fostered honest behavior, indeed, guaranteed it. For how can one have been successfully taught what is good and willingly reject it? We ignore the fact that the rhetorical obviousness of this question is a product of the active interpretation, which embraces appropriate conduct to begin with. The practical danger here is a confusion of verbal exhortation and tests with the effective development of moral conduct.

Let us return now to the further comparison of A and B statements. We have earlier seen that X's success in telling Y that such-and-such is the case does not require Y's learning that such-and-such is the case, whereas such learning is required for X's success in teaching Y that such-and-such is the case. Thus X may, for example, succeed in telling Y that Columbus discovered America without succeeding in teaching him that Columbus discovered America. We shall express this fact briefly by saying that A does not imply B. (It is, of course, understood that in every such comparison of two sentence forms, the two blank-fillers are to be taken as identical, the two 'X's are to be assumed to name the same person, and the two 'Y's are also to be assumed to refer to the same person.)

Is it, however, true that B implies A? If, for example, X is successful in teaching Y that Columbus discovered America, may we infer that X has succeeded in telling Y that Columbus discovered America? Many have appeared to hold such a view. They have seemed to picture a good part of the content of Y's learning as composed of facts or ideas impressed on his mind by his teachers, through some such activity as telling. Learning of facts has thus been construed as a kind of duplication by the pupil of ideas or statements originally produced by the teacher.[35]

Though many cases of teaching do indeed involve telling, the general inference from B to A seems unwarranted. Suppose, for example, the teacher does not actually tell the pupil that Columbus discovered America, but tells him only such things as allow him to infer it with the aid of other statements he is presumed already to

35. In this connection see, for example, Price, K.: On "having an education," *Harvard Educational Review*, 28:320 (Fall) 1958.

know. Suppose, even, that the teacher tells the student nothing of this sort, but arranges for him to read such texts as say or imply that Columbus discovered America. Suppose, finally, that the statements with which the student is confronted merely suggest but do not imply that Columbus discovered America. Must we in every such supposed case deny that the teacher has been successful in teaching the pupil that Columbus discovered America? Surely, there are many such actual cases in which we attribute successful teaching to someone who has not ever *told* the pupil what the latter has been successfully taught. Thus, B cannot be said to imply A. To say that X has told Y that so-and-so, is, roughly, to say something about X's actual utterances; it is to report some of these in indirect quotation. To say, on the other hand, that X has taught Y that so-and-so, is not to report X's utterances even indirectly.

We have noted that A does not imply B, since (briefly) B requires learning for success, whereas A does not. The force of this fact is that there are cases where learning does not take place, and hence where successful teaching does not take place, and where success in telling nevertheless does take place. It must not be thought, however, that whenever both learning and success in telling take place, success in teaching also takes place. The following example to the contrary thus provides another reason for denying that A implies B. Jones, let us imagine, is, on June 3, in the waiting room at the doctor's office. After some time, the nurse emerges to tell him that the doctor thinks it wise to skip the treatment planned for that day. She has, let us assume, been successful in telling him this. Let us, further, suppose that Jones not only hears it but learns it, and retains this bit of information for twenty years. (There are, it may be guessed, deep reasons for such learning, relating to Jones' psyche.) It is not likely that we should want to describe this situation by saying the nurse *taught* Jones that the doctor thought it wise to skip the June 3rd treatment, even though we are quite willing to say she told him the doctor thought it wise to skip the June 3rd treatment. Though learning in fact occurred here, the nurse was not trying to bring it about. She was, in fact, telling Jones something intended, on that occasion, to get him to leave the office. The learning that, in fact, occurred was not a sign of success in teaching, because there was no teaching, as normally understood. (It is a generally important fact, however, that what is said by X without intent to achieve Y's learning may, nevertheless, result in Y's learning.)

If we turn now, after this long discussion, to a consideration of the C (telling to) and D (teaching to) schemas, we shall be able to note both certain important analogies and important divergences with respect to the A (telling that) and B (teaching that) pair. As for the implication relationships between C and D, they are the same as those between A and B, i.e., implication fails both ways. Thus, one may succeed in telling someone to be honest without his learning to be honest, whereas one cannot succeed in teaching someone to be honest without his learning to be honest. Therefore, in cases where learning to be honest fails to occur, success in telling may still occur but not success in teaching. That is, C fails to imply D. There are, furthermore, cases where children have been successfully taught to be honest without having been *told* to be honest, as well as (at least some) analogous cases where they have been taught to be considerate, helpful, or friendly to others without ever having been *told* to be considerate, helpful, or friendly to others. If these cases are disputed, it will surely be agreed that some people have been taught to appreciate music without having been *told* to appreciate music. Any such case, once acknowledged, is sufficient to show that D fails to imply C.

Can we now construct, with respect to C and D, an example parallel to that of Jones' cancelled medical treatment, to show how the telling of something for some immediate purpose (not learning) may yet result in Jones' learning without involving teaching? The attempt to do so brings out some interesting divergences with respect to the A and B pair of schemas.

Imagine that Jones is waiting in the dentist's anteroom and that the nurse now succeeds in telling him to come into the office. We should hardly say she *taught* him to come into the office though she was successful in *telling* him to do so. But, unlike the earlier example, we cannot suppose that Jones *learns* to come into the office, either. To say that Jones learns to come into the office is normally to imply that there are several occasions involved, that is, it is to suggest some tacit 'whenever'-clause. But the terms of our example preclude such an implication in the case before us. The nurse is telling Jones to come into the office at the time of her utterance and no general 'whenever'-clause is attached. Jones either listens to her or does not, but he does not, in any event, learn to come into the office *on that single occasion*. (Correspondingly, he cannot be said to have been taught to come into the office on that single occasion.) There is a certain generality with respect to occasions of action that is normally required for 'learning to' and 'teaching to' statements, but that neither holds for 'learning that' and 'teaching that' statements nor for telling.

Some additional examples of this generality requirement may be welcome. In each of the following, the circumstances are such as to remove the likelihood of a tacit 'whenever'-clause, thus precluding the generality in question. While 'telling to' remains applicable, 'learning to' and 'teaching to' fail to apply. Consider first, 'She told him to open the window, as it was getting quite warm in the room.' The point of her telling relates to the momentary temperature; she is not telling him to open the window whenever it gets quite warm in the room, nor is she telling him always to open the window. Rather, she wants him to open the window now. Here, he may or may not open the window, but we would not say either 'He learned to open the window (then and there), as it was getting quite warm in the room,' or 'She taught him to open the window, as it was getting quite warm in the room.'

Consider, finally, 'He told them to wait for fifteen minutes,' said of a man leaving his friends to run an errand, not knowing if it would take more than fifteen minutes and so delay their common trip, or not. He tells them to wait for him only fifteen minutes and to proceed without him if he is not back by then. There is, in this case also, no 'whenever'-clause understood. He is not telling them always (whenever any occasion arises) to wait fifteen minutes or to do so always under specified circumstances. He wants them just this time to wait fifteen minutes. We cannot here say, no matter what they do, 'They learned to wait fifteen minutes (on that occasion),' or 'He taught them to wait for fifteen minutes.'

In these examples, 'telling' is quite appropriate but neither 'learning to' nor 'teaching to.' To say that X told Y to . . ., is, (as has previously been noted with respect to 'telling that'), to report $X$'s utterance indirectly; no matter what $X$ has said, general or specific in scope, such indirect reporting of content is feasible. To say, however, that $X$ taught $Y$ to . . . or that $Y$ learned to . . . is to say nothing by way of reporting $X$'s particular utterances; rather it is to say something of $Y$'s "patterns of action," running over more than a single occasion. It is to say what may be expected of $Y$ on other occasions if the learning is not somehow lost. If he has learned to stand whenever a lady enters the room, he may be expected to stand under those circumstances (unless he has somehow lost this learning in ways presumed independently specifiable). Thus, the generality of 'learning to' and 'teaching to' statements is something that has no direct counterpart in B statements and 'learning that' statements, whose blank-fillers do not (in every case) refer to what may be expected of $Y$. For example, '$Y$ learned that Columbus discovered America' does not say $Y$ may be expected to discover America at all; there is hence no place for a general specification of the conditions of such discovery.

It is thus easy to concoct a case such as Jones' cancelled treatment example, in which learning that . . . occurs, though the blank-filler is quite specific and is, moreover, told to him only to accomplish some particular purpose on a single occasion. When we try to get a similar example for 'learning to,' we find ourselves blocked by the generality requirement discussed. May we, however, find some other parallel to the cancelled treatment example? Let us, that is, begin by trying to fulfill the generality requirement and thus allow Jones to be spoken of as learning to . . . Secondly, let us find a circumstance in which he is told the same thing but without intent to achieve learning. We will then fail to have teaching though we have learning; we will, in short, have our desired parallel.

The difficulty is to fulfill all these requirements simultaneously. If we fulfill the generality requirement (say, Jones learns to come into the doctor's office *whenever* the red light flashes above the door) the problem is to suppose the nurse to have told him this without intending him to learn to come into the office whenever the red light flashes above the door. If she told him, however, she presumably intended for him to follow her instructions, but the following of *general* instructions is just exactly the learning to do certain things on particular occasions. If this argument is indeed correct, then a parallel example cannot be constructed at all for C and D. That the argument is sound is further suggested by the fact that, in the case just considered, Jones *may* reasonably be said to have been taught by the nurse to come into the doctor's office whenever the red light flashes above the door.

We have, then, come upon some important facts about C and D, notably relating to what has been called the 'generality requirement.' Both blank-fillers in C and D are imperative in grammatical form; imperative statements vary however in their degree of generality. 'Wait here for fifteen minutes!' asks for a certain action on the single occasion of its utterance, an action which may or may not be forthcoming. Learning is, however, not involved unless some general "pattern of action" under repeatable circumstances is understood to be in question, and where learning is not involved (even theoretically) teaching cannot be involved either. Thus, C, having no relation to learning, either as goal or as condition of success, may take either general or non-general imperatives in its blank, whereas D, clearly involving learning in both ways, takes only general imperatives as blank-fillers. The generality may, of course, not be explicit but only understood. Thus, in 'X taught Y to be honest,' it is understood that the imperative here is general, indeed universal: 'Be honest always.' In other cases, the context may make it clear that a non-universal, though still general imperative is involved, e.g., 'His mother taught him to say "thank you," ' may best be interpreted as 'His mother taught him to say "thank you" whenever he is given anything.'

In the sense illustrated by the various examples we have been considering, it may thus be said that teaching (to) involves *rules*,[36] rather than simply specific commands, and that the common confusion of these (as both stateable grammatically in imperative form) is a mistake. Specific commands are limited to the single situation. Though they may be issued by the teacher during the

36. For a different, though related, account of rules in teaching see Hare, R. M.: *The Language of Morals*. London, Oxford at the Clarendon Press, 1952, p. 56, reprinted in Scheffler, I.: *Philosophy and Education*, Op. cit.

teaching-interval, his goal is not merely to secure compliance on the unique occasions of their issuance. He wants his pupil to acquire "patterns of action" that will outlast the teaching-interval, that, in their stability, will render specific and continuous series of commands superfluous, even if conceivable. There is a world of difference between such "patterns of action" and compliance with specific commands, between the development of such "patterns" and the issuance of such commands.

Having compared B to A and D to C with respect to "implication" as above explained, we turn now to a cross-comparison of the two 'teaching' schemas B (teaching that) and D (teaching to). B clearly does not imply D nor does D imply B since the range of blank-fillers allowable in B and the range of blank-fillers allowable in D are different, as a matter of grammatical fact. 'X teaches Y that Columbus discovered America' becomes 'X teaches Y to Columbus discovered America' as we go from B to D, retaining B's blank-filler. On the other hand, going from D to B with D's blank-filler we get, for example, the transition from 'X teaches Y to be courteous at all times' to 'X teaches Y that be courteous at all times.' The second member of each of these pairs is not grammatical, and it remains ungrammatical when 'X teaches etc.' is changed to 'X is successful in teaching etc.' The first member in each pair is *not* ungrammatical, and is, moreover, often true. Furthermore, the change from 'X teaches etc.' to 'X is successful in teaching etc.' in the first member of each pair is likewise often true. Thus (roughly put), success with respect to either B or D does not carry with it success with respect to the other, where, as always, the same blank-fillers are concerned. Analogous considerations hold for A and C.

Nevertheless, there is a point of some interest to be noted by cross-comparison here. We have seen that B statements with norm-stating components are ambiguous and that, with an active interpretation, the success of the teaching to which they refer implies norm-acquisition of an appropriate sort. In certain cases, such norm-acquisition is expressed by statements of D form. For example, consider 'X teaches Y that one ought to be honest' in its active interpretation, according to which success requires Y's acquisition of the norm, i.e., his learning to be honest. In such a case, we may well say that to teach $Y$ that one ought to be honest implies teaching $Y$ to be honest. The implication here is not the sort we have heretofore discussed, inasmuch as the blank-fillers are different, and the precise specification of the range of B statements for which the present sort of implication holds is a problem not even attempted here. The reason for mentioning the implication at this point is to consider its bearings on moral education. For this purpose we need to consider just selected examples such as the above and, for instance, the implication from 'X teaches $Y$ that one ought to pay one's debts' to 'X teaches $Y$ to pay his debts.'

Of interest to moral education is the question whether the reverse implications hold in such examples. Does teaching $Y$ to be honest imply teaching $Y$ that one ought to be honest? Does teaching $Y$ to pay his debts imply teaching $Y$ that one ought to pay one's debts? (In both cases, let us, of course, give an active interpretation to the 'teaching that' clause.) Can one succeed in teaching $Y$ to be honest without succeeding in having $Y$ learn that one ought to be honest? Can $Y$, that is, learn to be honest without learning that he ought to be honest? Can he learn to pay his debts without learning that one ought to pay one's debts? These two latter questions are the crucial ones and are seen, upon reflection, to have affirmative answers. There are people who have, in fact, learned to be honest themselves but who have never learned that one ought to be honest, have never believed it, have even disbelieved it. There are people who have learned to pay their debts but who have never believed that one ought to pay one's debts.

To learn to be honest is to acquire a certain norm, a "pattern of action." Belief is not implied. The notion of belief is not even applicable. One learns to be honest but no one believes to be honest.[37] By contrast, to learn that Columbus discovered America is (whatever else is involved) to come to believe that he did. Similarly, to learn that one ought to be honest is to come to believe that one ought to, (whatever else is involved,—in this case, at least acquisition of the norm). To teach someone that one ought to be honest thus involves not merely teaching him *to be* honest (even

37. See Scheffler, I.: Comment, *Harvard Educational Review*, 28:337 (Fall) 1958.

for the active interpretation), but also trying to have him acquire the belief that one ought to be honest, (to acquire it within the restrictions of manner appropriate to teaching and discussed earlier). B statements may thus be said, in contrast to D statements, never to refer to the acquisition of norms solely, but also to some belief in the norm, some sort of intellectual acknowledgment of its authority. To teach $Y$ that one ought to be honest is thus not merely to try to get $Y$ to be honest; it is also to try to get $Y$ to be honest out of conviction.

The distinction here discussed is one of special importance to moral education. There are types of conduct or "patterns of action" that we want pupils to acquire, and concerning which we do not particularly care what rationales they adopt or even if they adopt any at all. Such, for example, are minimal forms of courtesy. There are sorts of conduct that we unhesitatingly support by reference to self-interest, for example, safety practices, preparation for some vocation. Moral conduct, on the other hand, is, in one important sense of the term, not merely behavior according to some independently specified norm, nor even such behavior governed by any rationale supporting the norm. Its rationale must, in a certain sense, be "objective," "impartial" or "disinterested" in its support of the norm. What this means is notoriously difficult to characterize, but it is reflected in the general and impersonal language of moral judgment (e.g., 'ought') which is normally used to express some rationales but not others. The rationale of a man's moral conduct, we may perhaps say, needs to be expressible by him in the language of moral judgment.[38]

One example may suffice to illustrate the point. Three people may all have learned to be honest, yet the first may be unreflectively honest because he has been reared in a protected environment where the option of acting dishonestly has never been allowed to present itself, the second may be honest because he believes honesty to be essential for advancement in his vocation or because he finds dishonesty emotionally taxing, while the third may be honest because he believes that one ought to be

38. An important paper, to which I am indebted for its treatment of these and related issues, is Frankena, W.K.: Toward a philosophy of moral education, *Harvard Educational Review*, Op. cit.

honest. The behavior of the first two conforms to the norm of honesty, but can hardly be characterized as moral (nor immoral) conduct, in the sense of the term we have here been considering.

If moral conduct is our goal in moral education, we are, in effect, striving to achieve not alone the acquisition of norms of a given sort in practice, but the reflective support of norms of this sort in an "objective" or "impartial" manner. To teach honesty as if it were a kind of safety rule or a conventional form of courtesy may effectively accomplish the first aim without in the least furthering the second. It cannot, on the other hand, be denied that a serious attempt to accomplish the second may delay and even impede the achievement of the first. (To encourage a *reflective and impartial* critique of norms may lead to a rejection of *our* norms.) We may, as teachers, try to further both aims by subjecting the very norms we are concerned with under the first aim to the sort of reflective scrutiny we encourage under the second.

We have previously established that C and D take imperatives as blank-fillers, and that C is an indirect report of someone's actual utterance. We have also seen that D does not imply C, that one may have been successfully taught to be honest without having been told to be honest, or have been successfully taught to appreciate music without having been told to appreciate music. We must now note that some of the imperatives allowable in C nevertheless carry with them the suggestion of X's unreasonableness in having uttered what they are being used (in C) to report indirectly; at the same time, no suggestion of X's unreasonableness is conveyed by their use within D contexts.

It is, for example, "unreasonable," in an important sense, to tell someone to appreciate music, to like Shakespeare, to understand the lot of the poor, since the things demanded by such tellings are not things one normally decides to do. Nevertheless, if someone in fact says to Y, 'Appreciate music!' 'Like Shakespeare!' or 'Understand the lot of the poor!,' his utterance may be reported by a C statement. The C statement, 'X told Y to understand the lot of the poor' is alright, merely reporting X's imperative, but (believing C), we feel X is unreasonable for having issued such an imperative at all.

The corresponding D statements, however, carry no corresponding suggestion of unreasonableness. (Compare 'X taught Y to appreciate music,' '. . . to like Shakespeare,' '. . . to understand the lot of the poor.') We may perhaps say that such examples reinforce the non-implication from D to C. For not only are some cases of successful teaching (as reported by D) not also cases of successful telling (as reported by C), but they are cases where such telling would suggest the unreasonableness of X. Not only have some people been successfully taught to appreciate Bach who have never been told to appreciate Bach in fact, but had they been told, their tellers would have been accounted unreasonable.

The independence of teaching from telling is underscored by such examples, at least for D and C cases. To teach someone to appreciate Bach, to understand quantum theory, to enjoy ballet, to sympathize with the downtrodden, is quite different from telling him to do so. He may indeed be told, but such telling is deemed unreasonable, where the corresponding teaching is not. Teaching, in fact, normally proceeds here not by the issuance of parallel imperatives, but by diverse other means through which such things as appreciation, enjoyment and understanding emerge and flower.

We have just discussed imperatives deemed unreasonable in asking for things that no one can decide to do. There is a weaker, relative sense in which imperatives may be unreasonable, though not unreasonable in the strong or absolute sense already discussed. This relative unreasonableness is, moreover, peculiarly important in connection with teaching. Suppose you, as teacher, were to give a list of elementary arithmetic problems to a boy and say 'Do these!' It cannot be said that you have asked him to do something that no one can decide to do. But it may very well be that *this* particular boy has not had the required arithmetic background (he was ill when the method appropriate to these problems was explained, and never learned how to do them). *He* surely cannot decide to do what you have asked him to do. Or imagine the (not strongly unreasonable) imperative 'Translate the passage before you into Greek!' addressed to a pupil who has not yet studied

Greek. *He cannot* decide to do what the imperative asks of him. The two imperatives of these two examples are unreasonable with regard to the persons to whom they are addressed and also to the times at which they are issued, respectively.

The relativity to time is important, for with appropriate learning the boy may be able to tackle the problems later, and the pupil previously unable to set about translating the passage into Greek may become able to deal with this task at a later time. Thus, imperatives not strongly or absolutely unreasonable may still be unreasonable to given pupils at given junctures, and this relative unreasonableness may depend, at least in part, on the nature of previous teaching. Where the appropriate teaching is successful, it thus serves to make whole hosts of imperatives reasonable to pupils, which had not been reasonable to them before. We had earlier seen that for strongly unreasonable imperatives as components of D statements, teaching normally proceeds in ways other than by parallel telling. It now appears that even where not strongly unreasonable imperatives are concerned, they may yet be unreasonable in particular circumstances, in which appropriate preliminary teaching (how) may serve to render them reasonable at a later date. Telling (to) is here shown not as a *way of* but rather as a *product of* teaching (how). (It is, of course, nevertheless true that telling, rendered reasonable by prior teaching, may in turn become a way of helping to teach new things or of strengthening old.)

We have, in the discussion just concluded, seen the importance of being able to decide to do what an imperative demands, and further, the dependence of such ability, in some cases at least, on having learned how to do what is demanded. The F (teaching how) statement is thus related to the C statement in that successful teaching how (reported by F) may render certain tellings to (reported by C) reasonable. These tellings to may, in turn, be ways of teaching to do the same things, but C, as we have seen, does not imply D. We must, now, systematically compare F with the other schemas, and in particular, with D.

It is easy to see that E (telling how) does not imply F (teaching how) nor does F imply E, even though, with complex skills, telling how may be more and more necessary to teaching how.

It is further obvious that B does not imply F nor does F imply B, as the blank-fillers of F are imperatives whereas the blank-fillers of B are indicatives. The important comparison here is that of F with D, for they are often confused, as we shall see in detail.

We must, at the outset, recognize that frequently a D form is used as abbreviation for an F form. To teach someone to do arithmetic problems is, normally, to teach him how to do them; to teach someone to swim is (as normally understood) to teach him how to swim. We are not here concerned with such abbreviations and, hence, when we refer to D, we refer to those D statements that are not equivalently rendered by corresponding F statements.

Perhaps, it will be suggested, there are none of this sort. But consider 'X teaches Y to pay his debts.' This statement is not (normally) replaceable by 'X teaches Y how to pay his debts.' The first may refer to character training while the second may refer to instruction in the proper use of checkbooks, money orders, and the like. Consideration of this example shows, moreover, that whereas teaching someone how to do something is sometimes necessary in order to teach him to do it, it certainly is not sufficient. Many people proficient in the proper use of checkbooks and analogous instruments of debt-paying nevertheless do not pay their debts, have not acquired the norm of debt-paying. F does not, thus, imply D, while D does not imply F either. For even if knowing how to pay debts is essential to paying them, to teach Y to pay them does not in every case involve teaching Y how to pay them; he may know how already.

F and D are distinct, we have said. For convenience, we may say (roughly) that D is concerned with norms and norm-acquisition, while F is concerned rather with skills and skill-acquisition. Often, in discussing subjects of the curriculum, we confuse the two. For example, we talk of "citizenship" as if it were a set of skills, whereas our educational aim is, in fact, not merely to teach pupils *how* to be good citizens but, in particular, to *be* good citizens, not merely *how* to go about voting, but *to* vote. We talk of giving them "the skills required for democratic living," when actually we are concerned that they acquire democratic habits, norms, propensities. To take another example, we talk of giving pupils the "ability to think critically" when what we really want is for them to acquire the habits and norms of critical thought.

Perhaps one motive for assimilating norm-acquisition to skill-acquisition is that skills are, in an important sense, morally neutral, while norms are not; skills require supplementary decision for their exercise, while norms characterize the very patterns of decision themselves. To extend the category of skills is, in effect, to seem to reduce the scope of the teacher's moral responsibility. Such responsibility cannot, however, be evaded by name-changing; it can only be hidden from view. The inculcation of habits, norms, and propensities pervades all known educational practice, and such practice is not therefore merely a matter of skills. Contrary to a dictum of Ryle's, teaching is *not* just deliberate equipping.[39]

The examples just considered illustrate a practical use of the schemas in clarifying curricular discussions. There are other such uses that will here be further illustrated. All hinge on the translation of abstract curricular talk into one or another specific form represented by our schemas. We may begin by citing Ryle's attempt to de-intellectualize our conception of skills, to deny that skillful performance is governed by explicit reference to rules or information.[40] To know how to swim is not to have memorized lots of swimming information and swimming rules to be consulted continually during the act of swimming. Information and rules may help initiate the learning of a skill, but the exercise of skill is not therefore to be identified with continued reference to

---

39. Ryle, G.: Op. cit., p. 310, reprinted in Scheffler, I., *Philosophy and Education*, Op. cit., p. 133. What is at issue is, thus, it seems to me, not whether inculcation of norms shall take place, but rather what norms shall be inculcated and in what manner, whether, e.g. our norms shall be restrictive or generous, authoritarian or democratic, whether they shall be dogmatically instilled by our educational institutions or whether they shall be taught, — explained and submitted to the independent judgment of pupils at crucial points during relevant teaching intervals. See, in this connection, Perry, R. B.: "Education and the science of education," in *Realms of Value.* Cambridge, Harvard University Press, 1954, reprinted in Scheffler, I.: *Philosophy and Education*, Op. cit., p. 15.

40. Ryle, G.: Op. cit., Chapter II, reprinted in Scheffler, I., *Philosophy and Education*, Op. cit., p. 92.

information and rules. To know how is something else, in short, than knowing that. Putting the point in this way makes it easy to see that Ryle is driving a wedge between B and F statements. To have such schemas before us and to try to translate our discussions of teaching and the curriculum into the specific forms they represent is likely to  make it easier to avoid the mistake Ryle is attacking.

In discussion of curricular aims, nothing is so easy and, at the same time, so confusing as the labelling of a whole area with some abstract noun. Translation of such abstract discussion into the particular forms of the schemas often poses questions of curricular choice hitherto concealed. For example, we frequently take "science" as an element of the curriculum and proceed to discuss "its" role and relative weight. Suppose we had to translate our ideas into B, F, and D forms. We should then be forced to clarify our aims with regard to this so-called element. Are we trying to teach that science is such-and-such, that it tells us this-and-that about the world? Are we rather trying primarily to teach how to think scientifically? Or are we really trying to teach our pupils to be scientific in their thinking and in their approach to problems? There is, of course, no suggestion here that one and only one question is to be answered affirmatively. The point is merely that the schemas compel the raising of such questions and, indirectly, the consequent ordering of values and choice of techniques required for answering them.

To take an associated example, "religion" is often taken as a curricular element and policy debates rage over the place of such an element. But the 'teaching of religion' is ambiguous. If we take it according to B (with fact-stating components), we construe it as $X$'s teaching $Y$ that religion is such-and-such, i.e., as, roughly, the giving of information relating to religion as a set of historical institutions, doctrines, and attitudes. If we take it according to D, we construe it as $X$'s teaching $Y$ to be religious, something quite different.[41] It is obvious that one may favor 'the teaching of religion' in either sense while opposing it in the other, consistently.

41. See White, M.: Religion, politics, and the higher learning, *Confluence*, 3:402, 1954, reprinted in Scheffler, I., *Philosophy and Education*, Op. cit., p. 244, and in White, M.: *Religion, Politics and the Higher Learning*, Op. cit.

To be clear about debates over religion in the curriculum requires elementary clarity with respect to the construction to be put on the phrase 'the teaching of religion.' In sum, the schemas that formed the basis for the discussions of the present chapter were intended both to provide important foci for analysis of the idea of teaching, and to be of some practical use in clarifying discussions of the curriculum.

# A FINAL WORD

A FINAL word may be put to the preceding discussions but no final word can be said on the problems with which they are concerned. For the tasks of philosophical clarification, like those of scientific inquiry, are endless. To complete an undertaking of either kind is immediately to be confronted with a variety of allied undertakings which cry for attention. We can, at this point, merely note what has here been done and try to place it in context by emphasizing its general framework and by relating it to questions that await further treatment.

In the first part of this study, we tried to analyze the logical force of three sorts of statement recurrent in educational discussion. We discussed various types of definition, addressed ourselves to educational slogans, and treated a number of pervasive metaphors of schooling. In each case, we developed certain general modes of handling the statements in question. Thus, for example, we distinguished stipulative, descriptive, and programmatic definitions, suggested independent consideration of the literal and the practical purport of slogans, and indicated the comparison of alternative metaphors as a way of determining their limitations as well as illuminating their common subject.

Throughout, we stressed the importance of context in determining relevant criteria of logical appraisal, with special reference to educational discussion which cuts across scientific, practical, and ethical spheres of human action. Accordingly, we warned, for example, against the uncritical transplantation of metaphors from scientific to practical contexts, and stressed the possibility of varying moral appraisal of the practical emphases of slogans in changing social circumstances. Accordingly, also, we pointed out that putting a scientific definition to programmatic use does not avoid but, rather, urgently requires independent moral evaluation of the program such use conveys.

In general, we repeatedly emphasized the significance of distinguishing practical and moral questions from others with which they are often confused. In this regard, for instance, we distinguished questions relating to a definition's convenience or descriptive accuracy from questions concerning the worthwhileness of the program it may convey. In this vein, too, we argued that criticism of slogans taken as literal doctrines and criticism of their parent doctrines need to be supplemented by independent appraisal of their practical purport and the practical movements with which they are associated.

Our main purpose in this first part of the book was to present general strategies for the critical appraisal of educational definitions, slogans, and metaphors, and to develop such categories and distinctions as might facilitate this appraisal. In attempting to achieve this purpose, we focussed on a variety of particular examples, dissecting such specimens not so much for their own sakes as for the sake of gaining insight into the logical anatomy of the species, though several of these specimens (for example, the 'organic' metaphor and the variant definitions of 'curriculum') have obvious direct interest of an educational sort.

It is therefore clear that what was done in these first chapters leads into a variety of specific questions concerned with the intensive study of further specimens of related types. The general categories and strategies here presented, that is, need to be applied to outstanding cases; they are perhaps best viewed as hypotheses for directing our analysis and criticism of such cases. As hypotheses, they do not pretend to finality; they are subject to refinement and revision in the course of application to further instances. Nevertheless, as in the case of other hypotheses, they organize our treatment of such instances, enabling us to get an initial grip on our material. To the extent that they facilitate the critical analysis of such material, they serve their purpose, even if they give way to more detailed and refined tools of analysis later on. What may, however, well be undertaken at present with their aid is the analysis, in depth, of specific clusters of definitions, slogans, and metaphors prominent in educational discussion, and the extension of such analyses to other sorts of discourse in education. Such analyses might well hope to achieve not only the clarification of urgent practical issues of educational policy, but also the clarification of fundamental assertions that figure in educational theory.

There is, it is clear, no readily available way of giving a systematic listing of such issues and assertions. We may, however, cite as a few *illustrative* problems for analysis: (a) the variant definitions of the academic subjects, of types of curricula, of intelligence and of achievement, (b) the slogans and counter-slogans involved in controversies over modern education, desegregation, scientific studies and the humanities, and academic freedom, and (c) the educational rôles of such metaphors as 'the ladder to leadership,' 'the several tracks of the curriculum,' and 'the control of learning'—a metaphor transplanted from psychology. Analysis of such problems in depth, relating the statements in question to others in surrounding discourses as well as to their respective educational contexts, may serve not only to bring out sharply the underlying practical issues awaiting decision, but also to enable assessment of the theoretical worth of constituent notions.

In the second part of our study, we concentrated in detail on the idea of teaching, discussing some basic characteristics of teaching as an activity and relating it to certain general features of educational research. We concluded this part of the study by dividing discourse involving the notion 'teaching' into three basic sorts and providing an extensive comparison with the notion 'telling,' focussing in some detail on issues relating to moral education. Our aim here was not only to throw light on 'teaching' as typically understood but to suggest how analogous treatment of curricular discussions might have helpful practical consequences in clarifying aims and policies.

Several features of our discussion of teaching are worth recalling at this point for their general interest. We emphasized the fact that teaching is a considerably narrower notion than that of fostering the acquisition of modes of behavior or belief, that it carries with it restrictions of *manner*, requiring acknowledgment of the pupil's sense of *reasons*. Teaching cannot, thus, we suggested, be assimilated to such psychological notions as 'setting up conditions under which learning will most effectively take place' nor to such social-scientific notions as 'acculturation' or 'transmission of the content of a culture.' The latter notions may be legitimate in certain scientific investigations but they blur those distinctions of manner which are fundamental to moral evaluation of educational policy.

We, further, distinguished "success" from "intentional" uses of the notion 'teaching' and showed how some controversies derive in part from lack of attention to this distinction. Concentrating on "intentional" uses of 'teaching' we interpreted the teaching referred to as an activity, denying that it must therefore be construed behavioristically as some pattern of bodily movement. We argued further that such a construction may independently be seen to be inadequate, and that learning to teach can thus not be taken to be a matter of mastering some distinctive pattern of movements.

Success in teaching, we argued, depends on factors outside of one's trying, and rules may be sought to render such trying most effective. Such rules are, in the case of teaching as in the case of seeking fruitful scientific theories, at best inexhaustive though helpful, i.e., capable of improving our effort though not capable of guaranteeing success. Improving the practical art of teaching through provision of appropriate rules is one main task of educational research, conceived not as some single science but as the overlap of several related scientific domains.

The degree to which teaching is supported by scientific research, we argued, is an important factor in determining its professional status. The continued development of such research and its application to teaching practice depends not only on the autonomous development of relevant sciences but on the continued willingness to apply such sciences to practice. It depends also, we suggested, on acknowledgment of the diverse orientations of teacher and researcher and on mutual understanding of their divergent goals.

Our comparison of teaching and telling led us to distinguish between them, in spite of their close relationships in practice. Discourse containing the notion 'teaching' we suggested be distinguished as involving either 'teaching that,' 'teaching to,' or 'teaching how to.' We emphasized that such norm-stating components of 'teaching that' statements as 'One ought to pay one's debts' are subject to a peculiar ambiguity as between active and non-active interpretations, depending upon whether or not conformity of conduct with the norm is required for teaching success. This ambiguity, we suggested, is dangerous in the sphere of moral education in encouraging the confusion of verbal exhortation with effective development of moral character.

'Teaching to,' we found, involves a certain sort of generality not required by 'telling to,' though both require imperatives for completion of their respective forms. Such imperatives cannot therefore be generally construed as specific commands or orders. 'Telling to' may involve such orders, aimed at securing immediate compliance, whereas 'teaching to' aims at developing stable and general patterns of action.

Such patterns of action, however, we suggested, do not exhaust moral education. For learning to be honest, we argued, does not in every case involve learning that one ought to be honest, coming to acquire a belief of a moral sort, coming to act honestly out of moral conviction. The distinction here is fundamental to moral education, for to ignore it is to run the danger of confusing the teaching of honesty, for example, with the teaching of safety rules or conventional forms of courtesy, while to acknowledge it is to be confronted immediately with the delicate educational problem of attempting to develop at once patterns of action and impartial reflection on such patterns.

With regard to imperatives, we argued that certain of these are strongly unreasonable in asking for things that no one can decide to do, and others are unreasonable in a weaker sense, in asking someone to do something which he, at the time, cannot decide to do. Such weak or relative unreasonableness may depend on gaps in prior teaching and, correlatively, where teaching how is effective, it renders whole hosts of imperatives reasonable for the first time. Thus, the issuance of imperatives is shown, here, not as a method of teaching but as something dependent, for its reasonable use, on prior teaching.

We argued, finally, that 'teaching how,' directed at skill-acquisition, is distinguished from 'teaching to,' directed at norm-acquisition, and we suggested that expanding the scope of the former at the expense of the latter is often a way of evading responsibility for those norms of action toward which teaching is, in fact, directed. To translate curricular proposals, in cases where this distinction is relevant, into one or the other of the forms mentioned, is a way of pinpointing the issues involved. Analogously, to employ the three schematic forms of 'teaching' in other curricular deliberations may help us in clarifying our aims and in evaluating the decisions at stake.

As in the case of the general strategies presented in the first part of the book, the considerations presented in the second part lend themselves to applied uses with respect to cases not here discussed. The question of manner involved in the notion of teaching may, for example, be pursued with regard to other alternative conceptions of teaching than the psychological and social-scientific ones mentioned above. So also, the distinctions between "success" and "intentional" uses, between exhaustive and inexhaustive rules, between active and non-active interpretations, and between reasonable and unreasonable imperatives may well be applied to a variety of educational issues not here treated.

As in the case of the first part of the book, too, the examples we *have* treated have their own direct educational interest. Thus, for example, our critique of "behavioristic" interpretations of teaching and of teacher education, our emphasis on acknowledgment of the pupil's sense of reasons, our treatment of educational research, and our analyses of moral education bear on several important issues in educational theory.

There are, however, a whole set of questions that require investigation, not in the sense of applying notions here developed but rather in the sense of exploring different, though related, territory. We have, after all, concentrated on the idea of teaching. Other educational ideas urgently require analysis as well. Thus, for example, the notions of discipline, maturity, learning, understanding and explaining, which approach the philosophy of mind as well as the philosophy of knowledge need to be looked at from the perspective of education. Equally, the notions of authority, responsibility, and institutionalization of conduct, which approach the philosophy of morals as well as social philosophy, could profitably be analyzed from the vantage point of educational concerns.

Such investigations, as well as the applications mentioned earlier, may well lead to revision or refinement of the conceptions presented in the body of the present study. These conceptions, it must be repeated, are presented throughout as hypotheses, with no claim to absoluteness, self-evidence, or finality, but rather in the hope that they will further critical analysis of the problems of education.

# INDEX